KUALA LUMPUR
PANORAMA

MANAGING EDITOR martin cross
DESIGNER vani nadaraju
PRODUCTION MANAGER sin kam cheong

FIRST PUBLISHED 2011 BY

EDITIONS DIDIER MILLET PTE LTD
121 telok Ayer street #03-01
singapore 068590
telephone: +65 6324 9260
facsimile: +65 6324 9261
email: edm@edmbooks.com.sg
website: www.edmbooks.com

EDITIONS DIDIER MILLET SDN BHD
25 jalan pudu lama
50200 kuala lumpur, malaysia
+603 2031 3805
+603 2031 6298
edmbooks@edmbooks.com.my

©2011 editions didier millet pte ltd
Printed by Tien Wah Press, Malaysia.

All rights reserved. No part of this publication may be reproduced, stored in a retrieval system, or transmitted in any form or by any means, electronic or mechanical, including photocopying, recording or any information storage and retrieval system, without the prior written permission of the publisher.

isbn: 978-981-4260-04-6

COVER The vista looking from one Petronas Twin Tower to another. BACK COVER View across the Kampung Attap area to three of the city's architectural landmarks: Menara Maybank, KL Tower and the Petronas Twin Towers.

Kuala Lumpur Panorama was made possible thanks to the generous support of

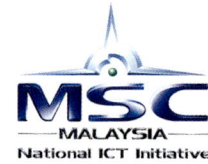

KUALA LUMPUR
PANORAMA

PHOTOGRAPHY S.C. SHEKAR
with YEE FAN
TEXT AMIR MUHAMMAD

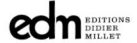

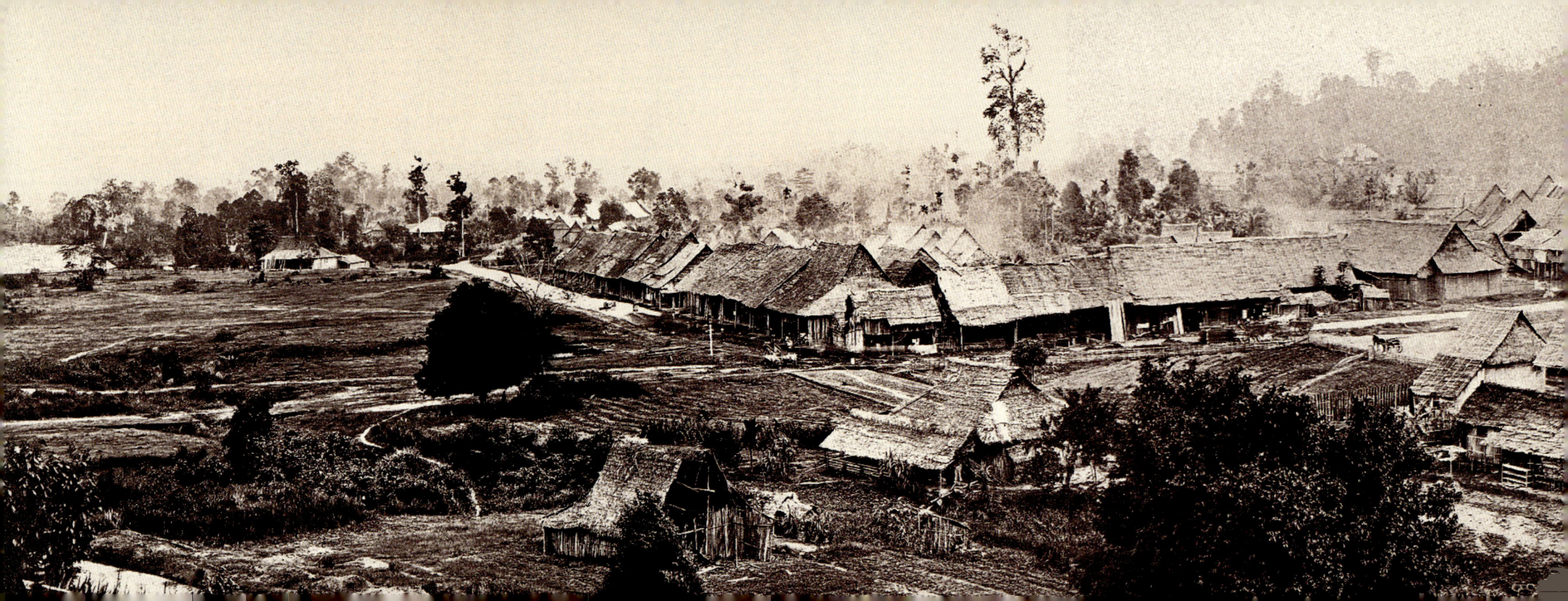

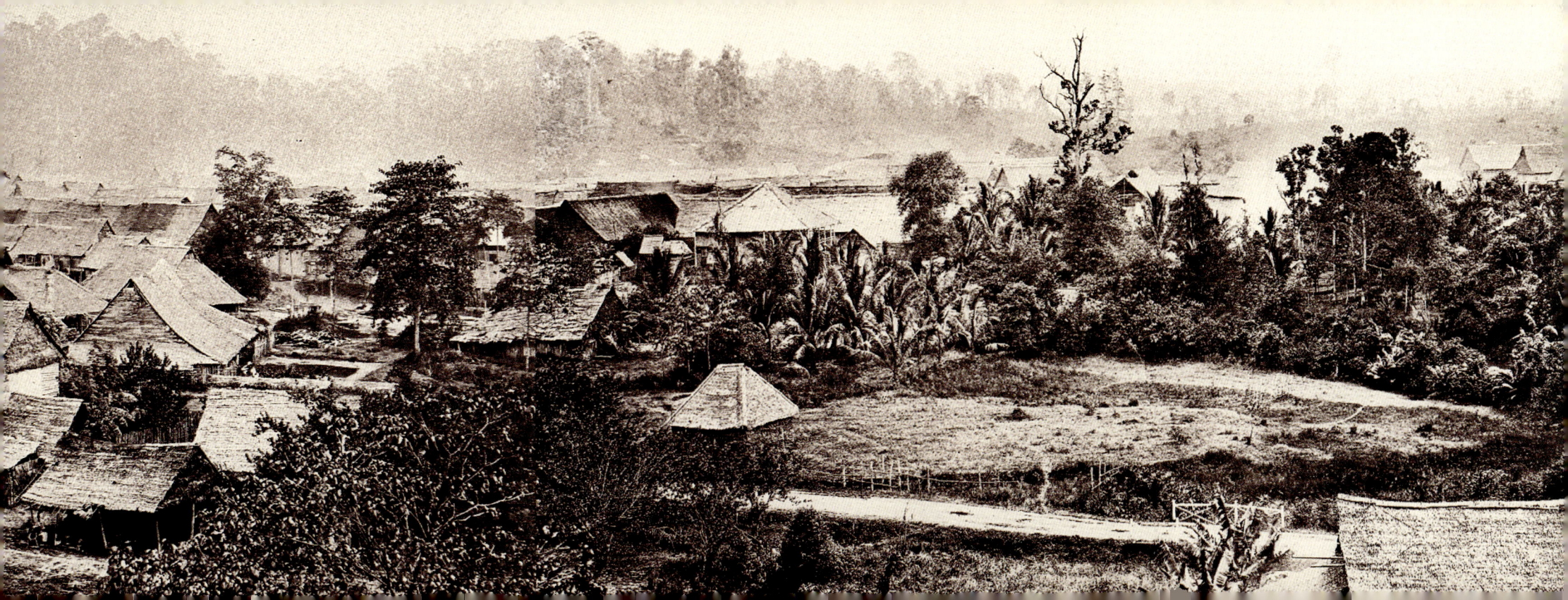

CITY OF MUD

My favourite novel about Kuala Lumpur is told primarily through pictures, and is cartoonist Lat's *Mat Som* (1989). The titular protagonist, a young writer who is frequently broke, starts off in typically modest style by saying that he doesn't know how to introduce himself—in a city like this, people like Mat Som tend to get lost—and so begins with his name, and that of his father.

So, then, we will start with the city's name. Kuala Lumpur started off as a place for tin-mining in the mid-19th century. The name means 'muddy estuary' and marks the meeting-place of the Klang and Gombak rivers. Today, that spot is marked by one of our oldest and prettiest mosques, Masjid Jamek. As for the father's name, there is some dispute. For decades, Malaysians thought of Yap Ah Loy, the third Kapitan China (Chinese Captain) and thus town headman, as being the founder of Kuala Lumpur. He was in office from 1868 to his death in 1885. Starting in the 1980s, there were suggestions that paternity be awarded instead to Raja Abdullah, the Malay aristocrat who led a team of tin miners upriver from Klang,

PAGES 4–5 Kuala Lumpur, photographed by G.R. Lambert & Co. in 1884.

THIS PAGE The place where the Gombak and Klang rivers meet, giving Kuala Lumpur ('Muddy Estuary') its name, although almost most KL-ites would be unable to tell you which river is which. Lying between the two rivers are the modest white onion domes of one of the city's oldest mosques, Masjid Jamek, completed in 1909.

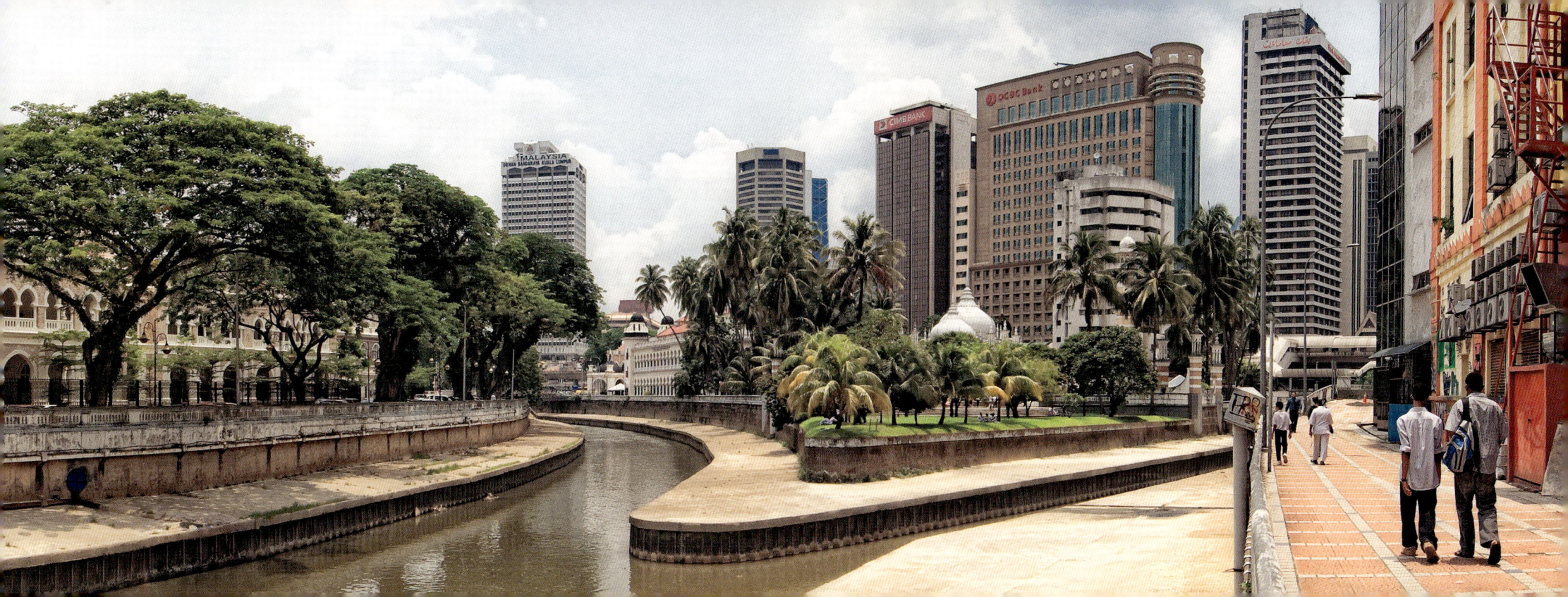

> "Malaysians have a robust ethnic humour based on stereotypes, which can be summed up by a line from Huzir Sulaiman's satirical play 'Atomic Jaya' (1999): "The Chinese do the work, the Malays take the credit, and the Indians take the blame."

which was then the state capital of Selangor. This happened in 1857 and, although most of that first expedition succumbed to malaria, this started the commercial exploitation that turned Kuala Lumpur into the town that would become the national capital a century later. The choice between these two men, as any Malaysian can tell you, strikes at something very fundamental: Was the city founder an ethnic Chinese or an ethnic Malay?

In 1880, Yap Ah Loy was the largest land-owner in the place, and owned half of all property. Today, the road named after him is, at 80 metres, the shortest in the city. The bigger insult is that his name is now not featured in Malaysian school history books. He was there when I was at school in the 1980s, but things are different now. Would he even like this place if he were to emerge, either through resurrection or the magic of CGI? There's hardly any opium, and he'd need to travel an hour outside KL (which is what everyone now calls it), to Genting Highlands, to be able to gamble legally—and even this would be the tamer Western-style gambling, where a dress code is enforced, rather than the more raucous Chinese games played on premises he earned part of his living from.

The road named after Raja Abdullah, meanwhile, is stuck in the least developed area of the city, Kampung Baru. This area was gazetted by the British as Malay Reserve Land and ownership is tied to ethnicity. The monarchy (the Raja in his name signifies royalty) still exists; the brand-new National Palace is a massive, expensive complex in a residential suburb. It is taking the place of the current Palace, which used to be the house of a Chinese tycoon. So, once again, a variant of the earlier question arises: Should the King, who symbolises Malay customs and values, be living in a house built by a Chinese?

Malaysia is one of the most racially conscious societies in the world. Many foreigners may think 'Malay' and 'Malaysian' are the same thing, but the former is an ethnic grouping that is linked with political power, and comprises about 60% of the citizens who go by the latter name. There is a political establishment based on ethnic-based parties and, more cheerfully, Malaysians have a robust ethnic humour based on stereotypes, which can be summed up by a line from Huzir Sulaiman's satirical play 'Atomic Jaya' (1999): "The Chinese do the work, the Malays take the credit, and the Indians take the blame." The packed audience that I saw this with laughed uproariously at the line, a laughter with the cringe of recognition.

Economic power is associated with the Chinese, although the government's ameliorative-action economic policies from the 1970s created a thriving Malay middle-class, and a few billionaires to boot. As in most of the bigger Malaysian cities, the Chinese comprise more than half of KL's population. Cantonese is the most widely spoken language here, but most non-Chinese never feel the need to learn it. One of the most famous shopping areas has been called Petaling Street for over a century—at the bustling markets, you can get fake Rolexes and genuine exotic meat—but the Chinese have always called it a different name: *Shu Chong Kai* (Tapioca Factory Road, because Yap Ah Loy built one there). It's the same place, but it's claimed in a different way.

The British, who administered the city from its tin-mining beginnings to national independence in 1957, made full use of these ethnic divisions: if everyone were slightly suspicious of one another, there would be no united anti-colonial rebellion. Aside from race-based politics, a prettier colonial legacy is the buildings. The old administrative district which consists of the beautiful Sultan Abdul Samad building and its surroundings was, up to 1998, the most iconic section of KL. When lit up at night, it's a fairy-tale of mock-

Moorish and mock-Tudor architecture. Cricket used to be played at the Selangor Club *padang* (field). The Club was nicknamed the Spotted Dog and the most likely origin of this phrase is, yet again, racial: it was a predominately white establishment that allowed a few non-whites. There's also the old Anglican church, where the dress code used to be very formal. Fast forward a few decades, and the area around the church became famous for a different kind of costumed congregation: transvestites. They got chased away, and were replaced after a fashion by mat rempit, a slang term for the illegal motorbike racers who, in the early 2000s, made nocturnal KL very noisy. It's the same place, but it's claimed in a different way.

Roads are constantly being renamed—in the nationalistic 1980s, many English names were replaced by local ones—a sign of a city always, to use a term not popular then, 'rebranding' itself. The biggest rebrand was completed in 1998: the 452-metre Petronas Twin Towers, then tallest in the world, dominated the skyline and virtually demanded to replace the Sultan Abdul Samad building as the postcard image of KL. "It's Mahathir's biggest erection," went the joke then, and its whole concept was tied with the go-getting era of the country's fourth Prime Minister. It's a two-finger salute to the world. As a tourism destination,

> "As in most of the bigger Malaysian cities, the Chinese comprise more than half of KL's population. Cantonese is the most widely spoken language here, but most non-Chinese never feel the need to learn it."

"KL started small and was allowed to sprawl, sometimes messily, in all directions. Putrajaya, on the other hand, was deliberately constructed to be neat and imposing."

KL had always lagged behind the two nearest capitals: Bangkok had more licentious thrills and colourful customs, Singapore was better at packing its melting-pot diversity into cute boxes. Now, with the KLCC (Kuala Lumpur City Centre) towers, Malaysians didn't have to feel that inferior.

Tellingly, the initial site for the towers was rejected because the soil was not suitable; it's as if the ground resisted such uncharacteristic grandiosity. Even more tellingly, KLCC is also a shopping mall. Shopping is pretty much what defines us. One of the most poignant photographs in this book is of people posing in front of a giant Lat cartoon situated in, yes, a shopping mall. I know this sounds pathetic, but for us KL-ites born in the 1970s onwards, many of our earliest memories are tied to shopping malls. The air-conditioning is colder than necessary, but everyone is used to it now. The burka-clad Arab women—who have been coming here as tourists with their families since the 9-11 attacks made visits to Western countries difficult—appreciate them, too.

There are very few public spaces in which you aren't expected to spend money. There was a 'moral panic' in the 1980s about *lepak* (loitering), which simply meant young people who wanted to hang out but didn't have the money to shop. Food, however, is plentiful and cheap. The first thing that any Malaysian misses when going abroad is the multiethnic megamix of cuisine that can be obtained at any hour of the day, as well as the iconic *teh tarik* (milky 'pull tea') beverage that is exactly the same colour as the two rivers where KL started. It's at the eateries—often late at night, when things are not too humid—that gossip is exchanged, new friendships are formed, business deals are conducted, and waistlines are subtly expanded. You can say that food is the unofficial religion of Malaysia.

    The pretty face of the real official religion, Islam, can be seen in the National Mosque (built in 1965). Unlike most mosques built later, it doesn't try to look Arabian. There isn't even a dome, which has been a cliché of Malay-Muslim 'power architecture', especially since the city of Putrajaya became the seat of government in 1999. KL started small and was allowed to sprawl, sometimes messily, in all directions. Putrajaya, on the other hand, was deliberately constructed to be neat and imposing. Although its dominating architecture and wide-open roads make it a favourite for TV commercials, it's safe to say that everyone prefers KL. True, KL's identity isn't a bold, fixed one: it is a city named after mud, after all.

Mud is earth plus water. Two massive floods (in 1926 and 1971) brought life to a standstill. Despite the allegedly flood-mitigating powers of the SMART tunnel (completed in 2003), floods still occur. If you are stuck in one of the city's notorious traffic jams during a downpour, you might entertain an apocalyptic fantasy of everything being swallowed by nature, for KL to regress back into the malarial jungle that it was only a century and a half ago. Unlike most capital cities, KL is not a sea-port. Even tin, the city's initial *raison d'etre*, is now used mostly as part of the pewter alloy, which is fashioned into touristy souvenirs. So, in the strictest sense, it's not a city that *needs* to exist; indeed, Putrajaya has taken over national administrative duties. And every KL-ite spends so much time complaining about KL (the traffic, the pollution, the red tape, the rising crime), that it might serve us right if it did disappear altogether.

    One of my favourite photographs from S.C. Shekar's evocative collection in this book is the very last one. It's of one of the first things an overseas visitor at the KL International Airport (completed in 1998) sees, and it's a fantasy of a neat jungle literally encased in glass and steel. As if nature could be contained and therefore tamed so easily! But it is actually the nature of the people who have built, and continue to build, KL that is being unconsciously represented here, people who are resilient and will continue to grow even in a place that seemed, initially at least, to be inhospitable.

It was said of the 15th-century port of Malacca that, if you were to stand in just one place, you could hear 300 languages being spoken. This, in less exaggerated form, is true of KL today. There are hundreds of thousands of migrant workers, documented and undocumented, and they have changed the landscape for good. They take jobs that Malaysians are too lazy or pampered to do, such as serving in 24-hour mamak (Indian Muslim) eateries. Then again, everyone in KL in the late 19th century was an immigrant. A song quoted on the last page of *Mat Som* contains the question "Do you want to be New York?" To a socially conservative Malaysian, New York would seem like a den of iniquity. But I prefer to answer: "Yes, I want to be in a city where everyone comes from elsewhere; therefore, everyone owns and shapes it to become something much greater than the sum of our individual origins."

Amir Muhammad, Kuala Lumpur, August 2010.

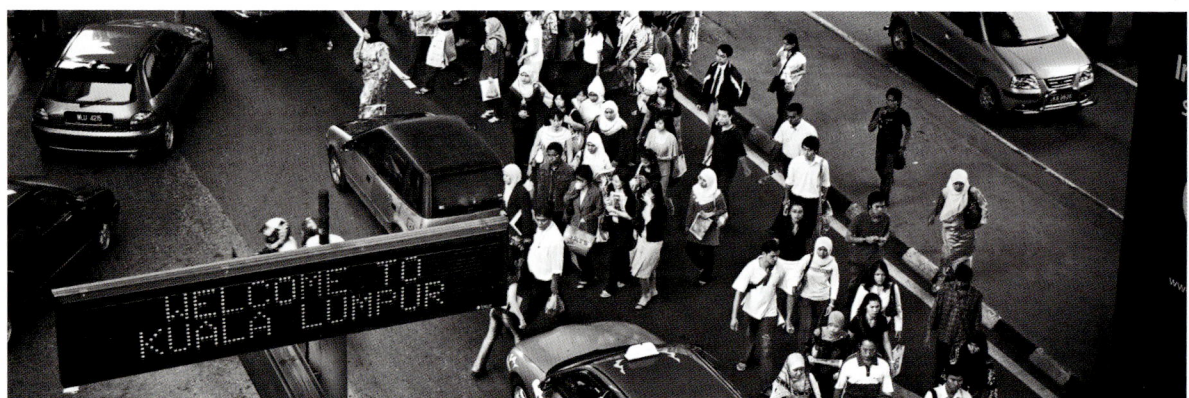
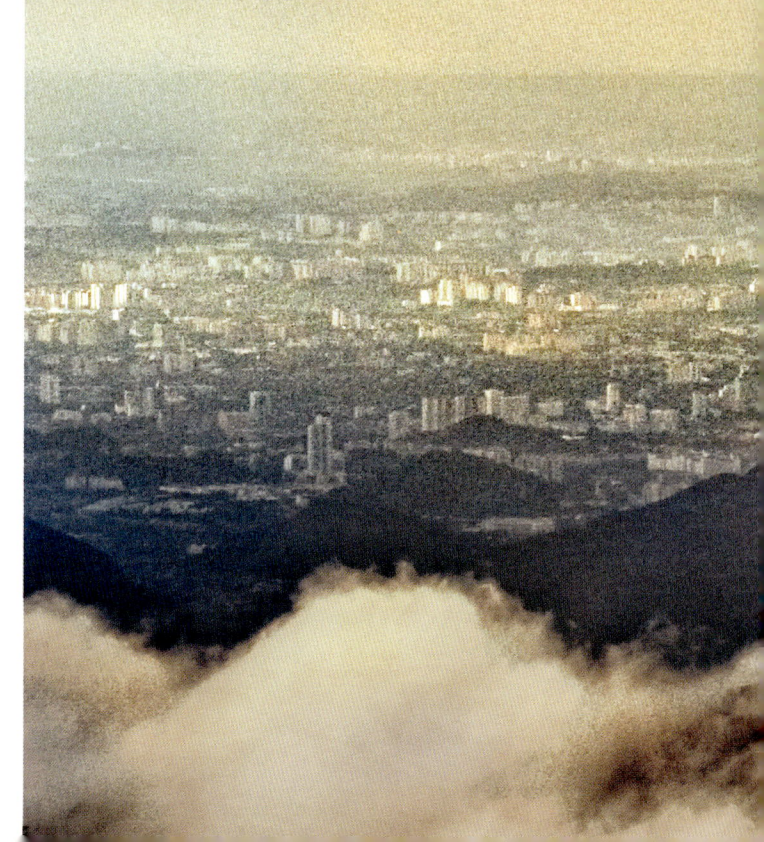

THIS PAGE Pedestrians at Jalan Tun Perak, next to the Masjid Jamek LRT station, are greeted by a Town Hall electronic display board. OPPOSITE View from Genting Highlands of a city a century and a half in the making.

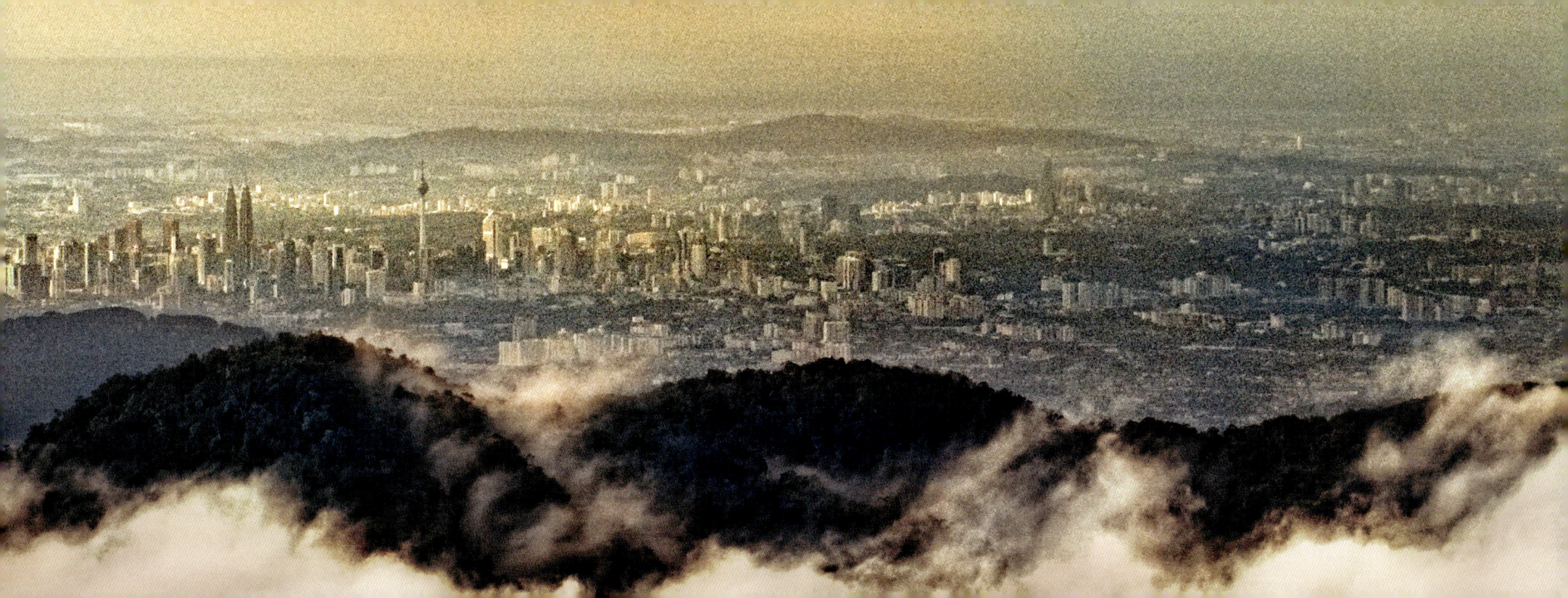

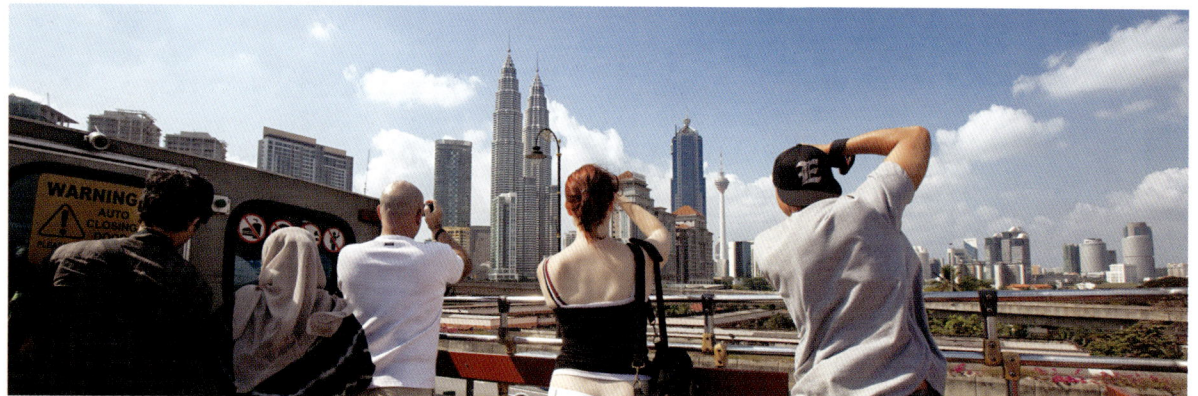
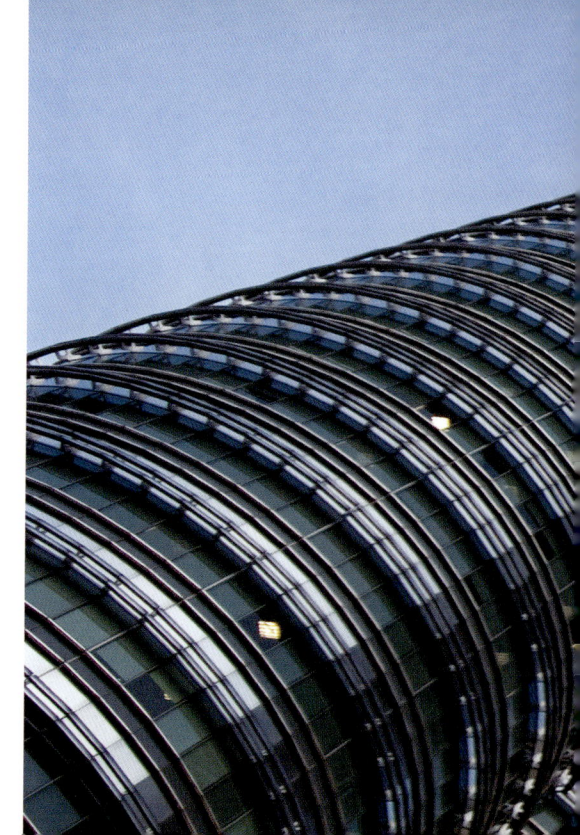

THIS PAGE AND OPPOSITE The Petronas Twin Towers, or Kuala Lumpur City Centre (KLCC), pipped the Sears tower in Chicago in 1998 to be declared the world's tallest. Particularly controversial (especially to people in Chicago) is the fact that the 60-metre spires on top of the towers were taken into consideration when measuring the height. The towers have dominated the KL skyline in a way no previous structure has.

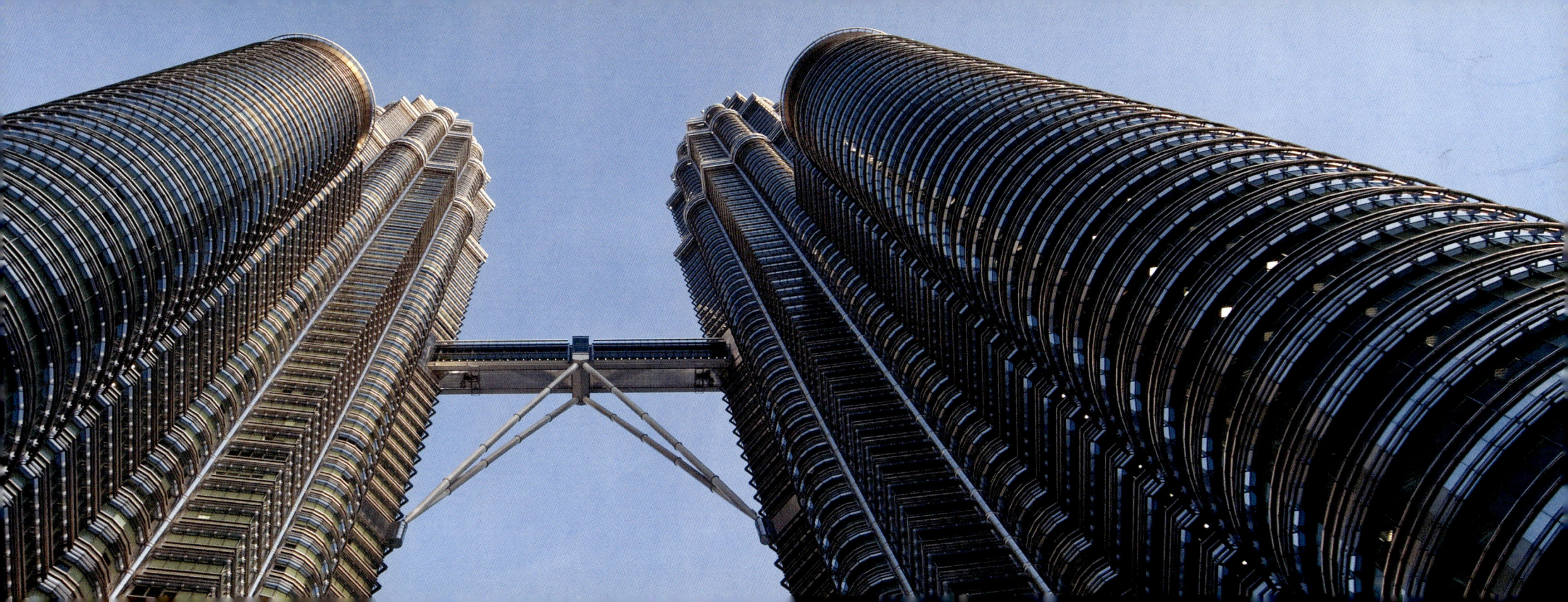

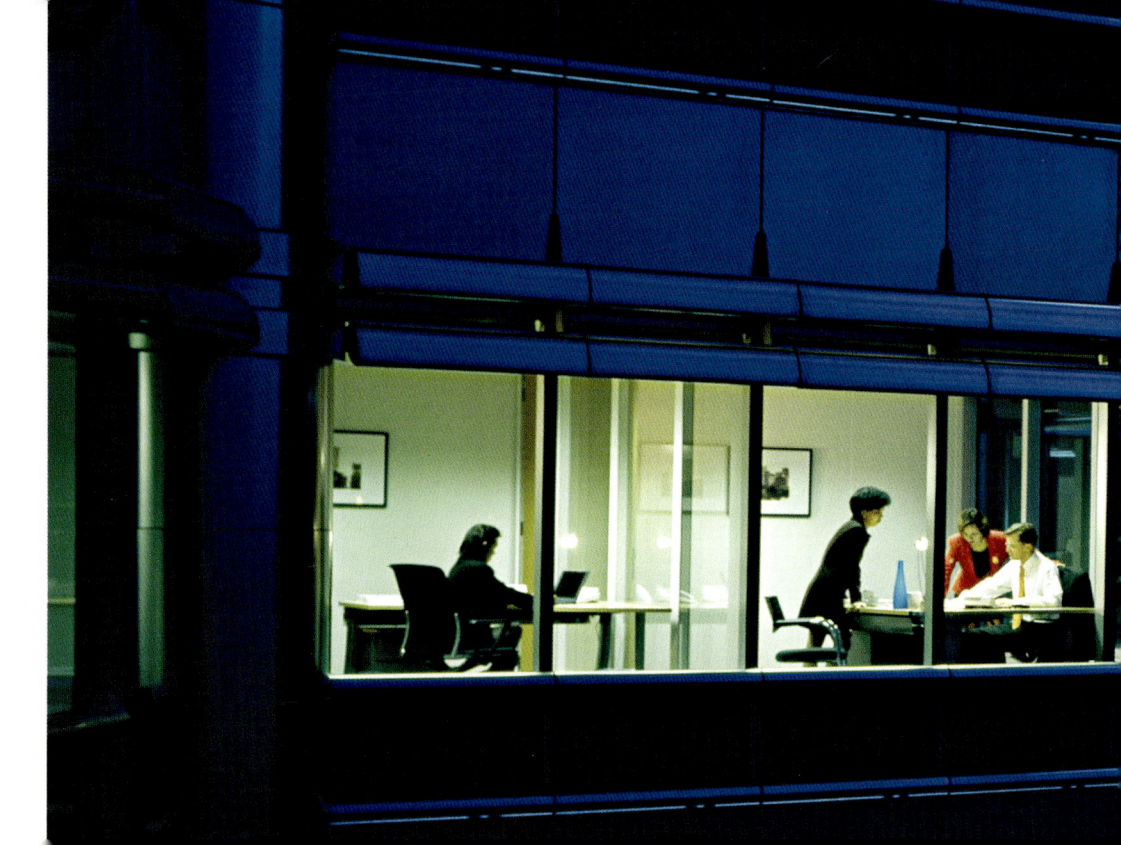

THIS PAGE New York-based architect Cesar Pelli designed the Petronas Twin Towers to be connected at the 41st and 42nd floors. This 'sky bridge' is open for tourists – but only during the day.

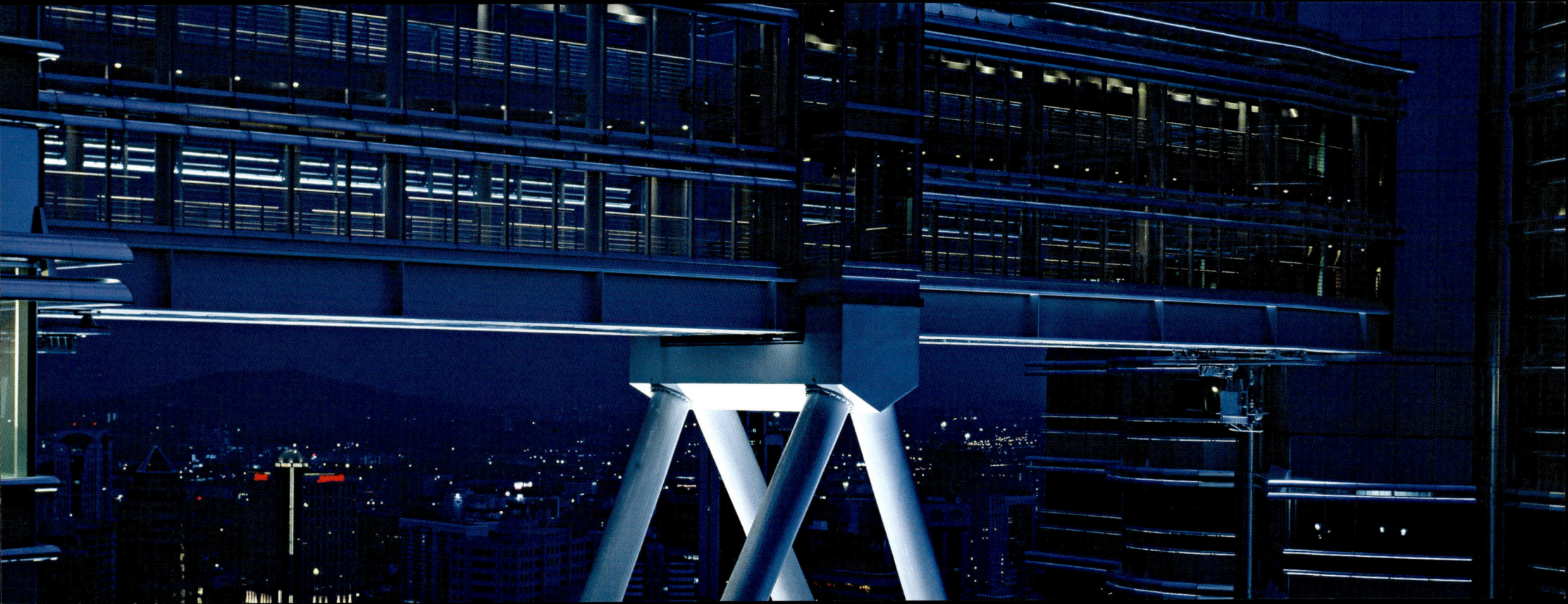

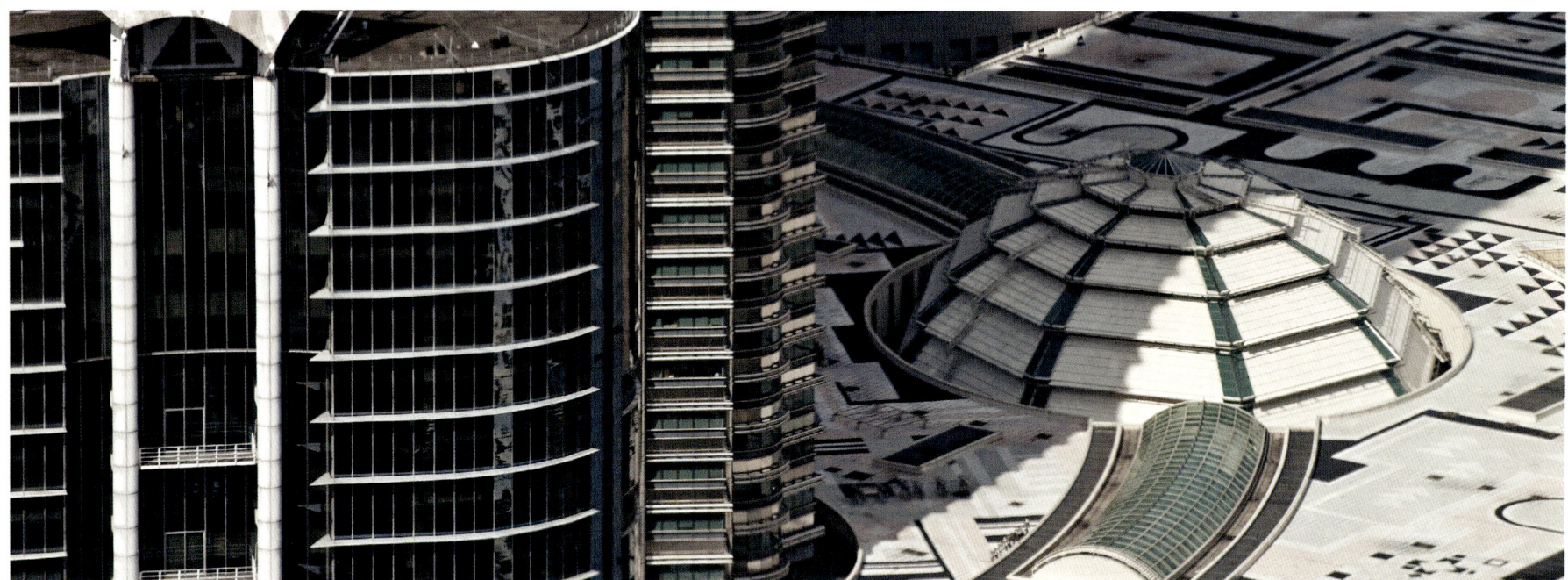

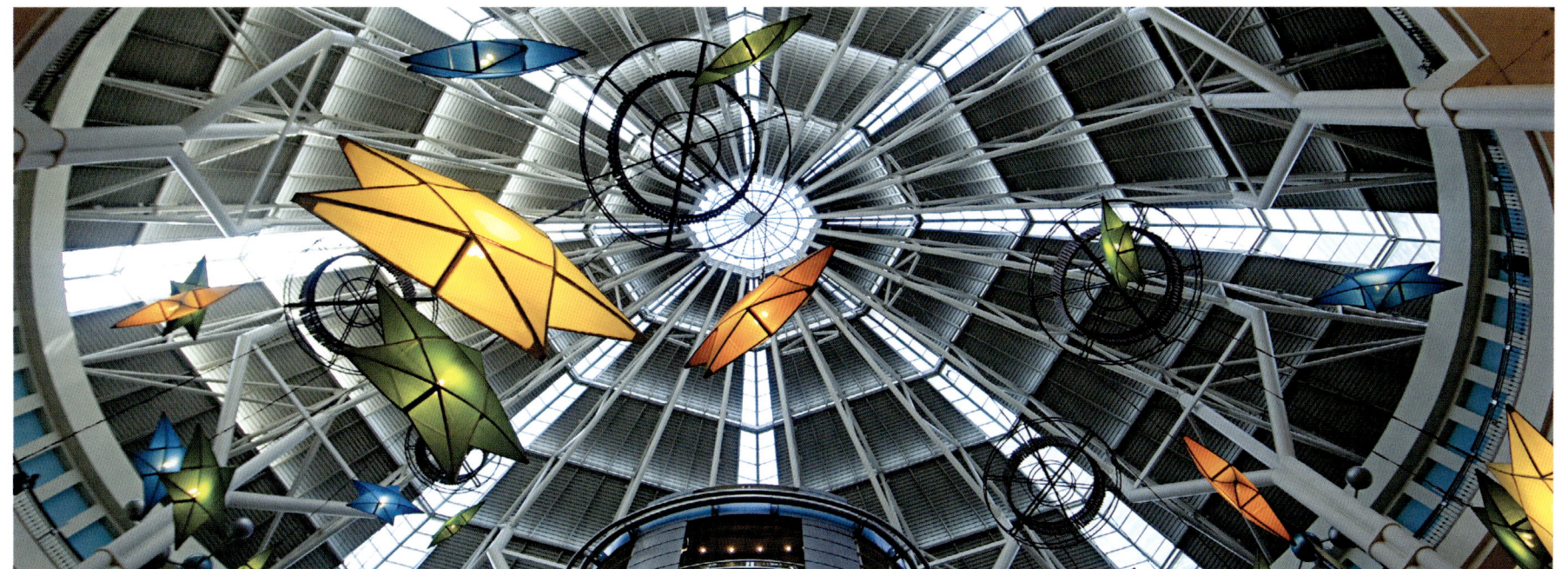

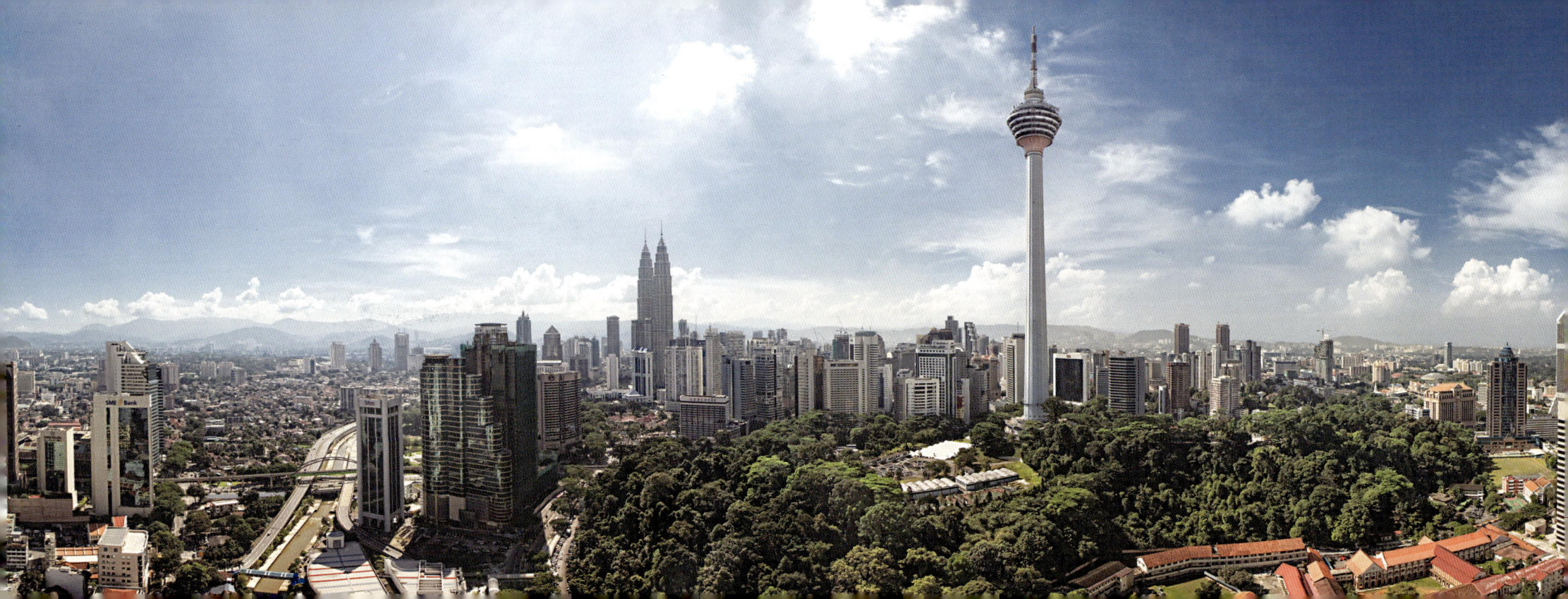

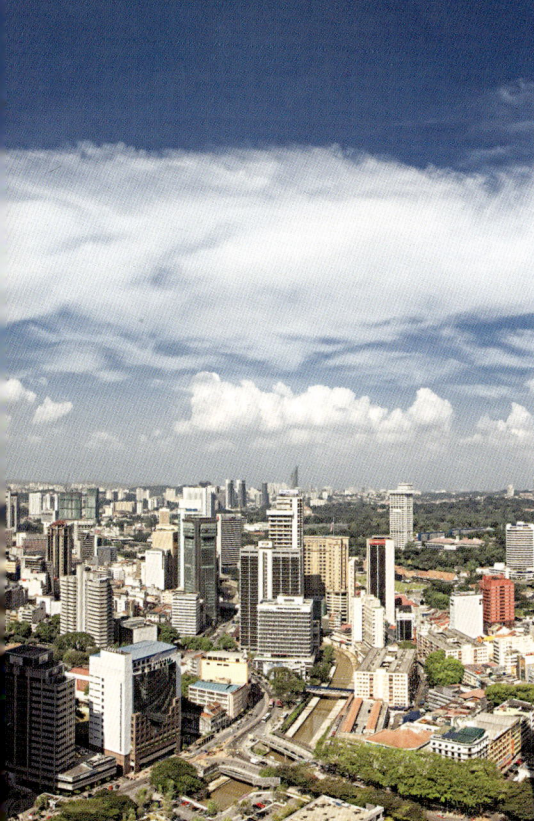

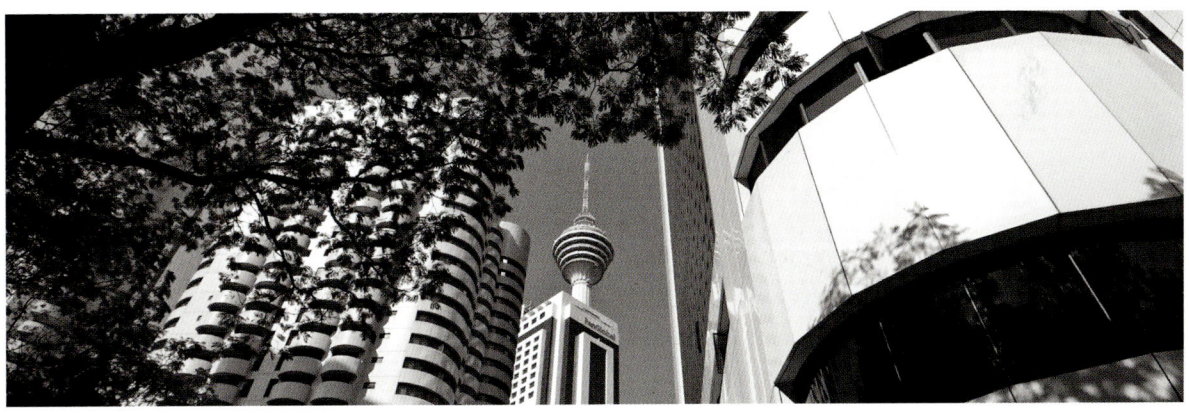

PAGES 22–23 The roof of the Suria KLCC shopping centre – as seen from the sky bridge and looking up from inside the shopping centre. THIS PAGE During its construction, the Menara Kuala Lumpur (KL Tower) was billed to be the world's third tallest telecommunications structure. By the time it was unveiled in 1996, a brand-new tower in Shanghai had actually beaten it to third place. This didn't stop the unveiling from being marked by the world's longest fireworks display. The tower has since blushed pink with pleasure. OPPOSITE KL Tower is on Bukit Nanas ('Pineapple Hill'), probably the only green lung left in the commercial heart of KL.

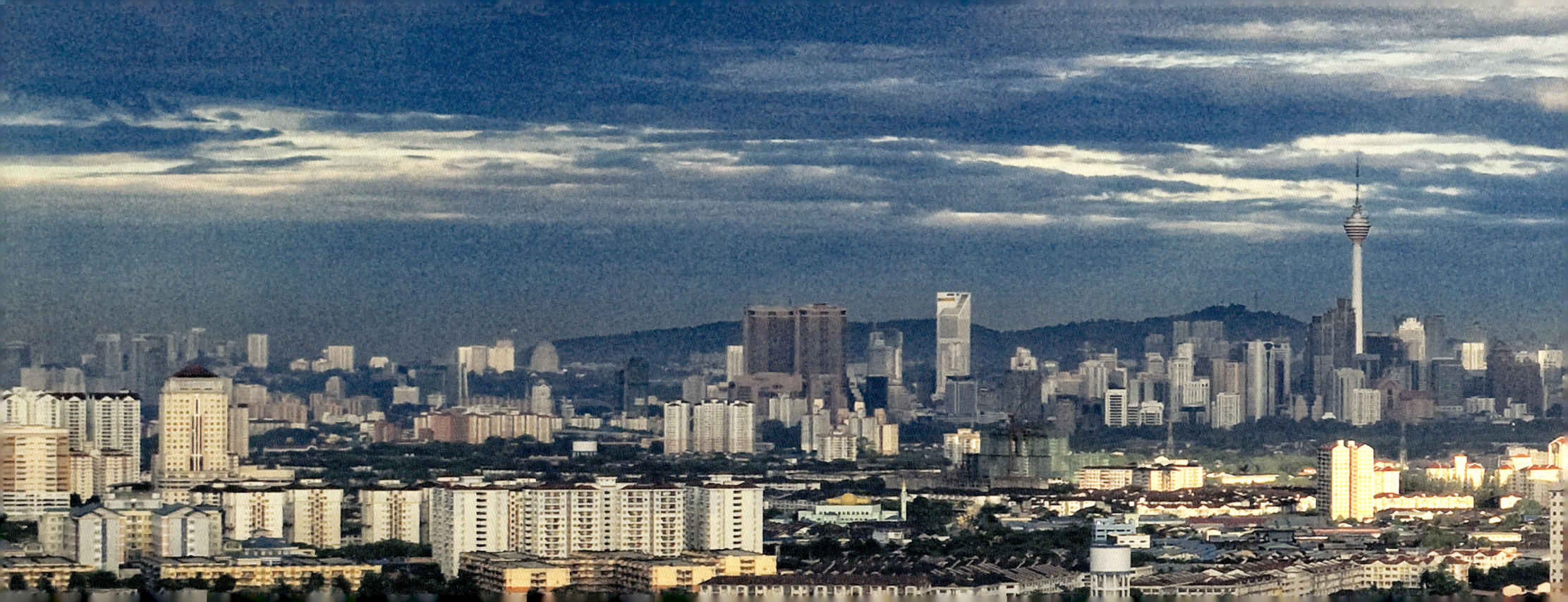

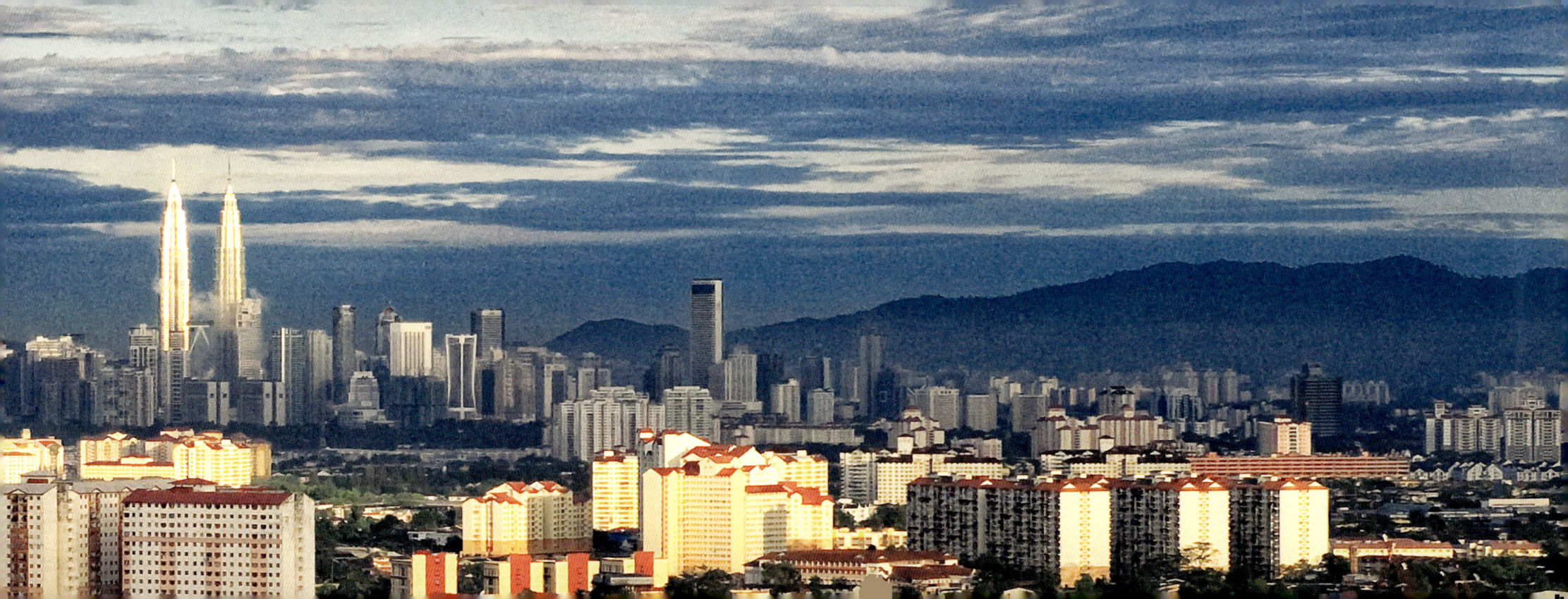

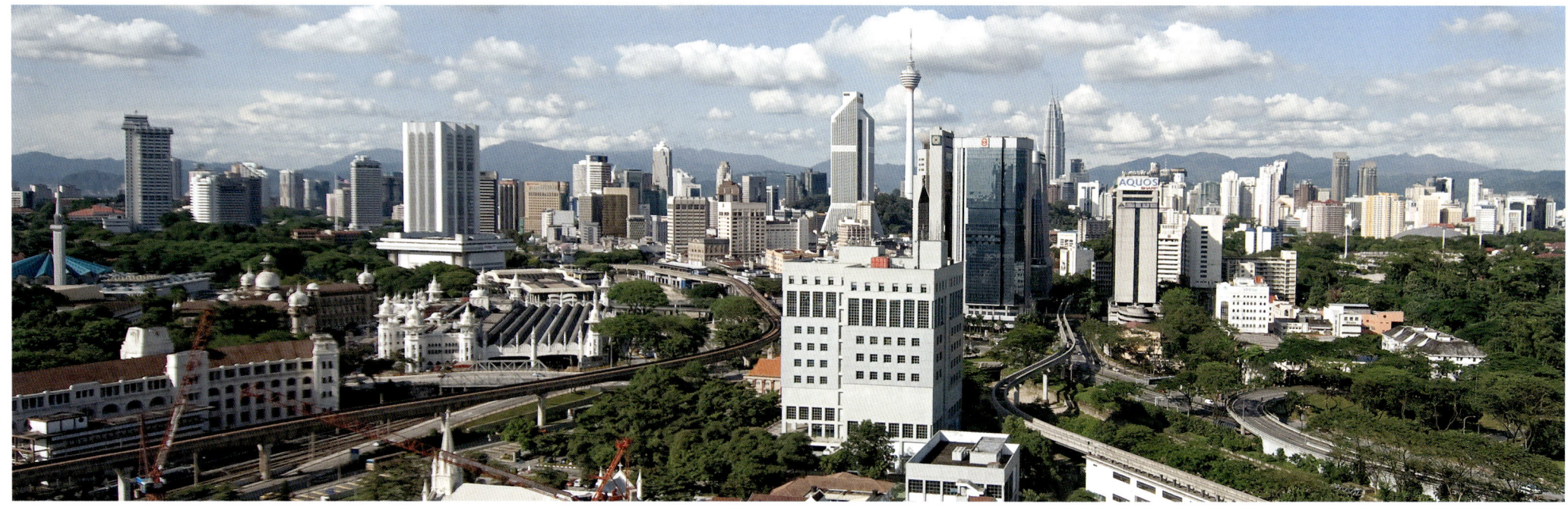

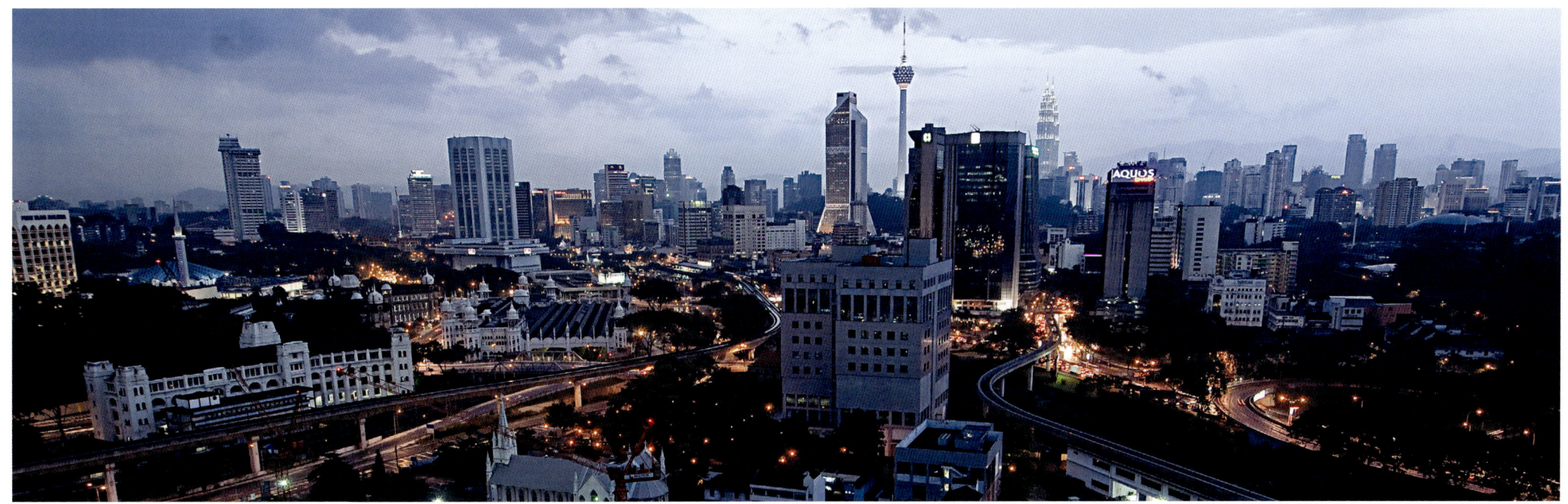

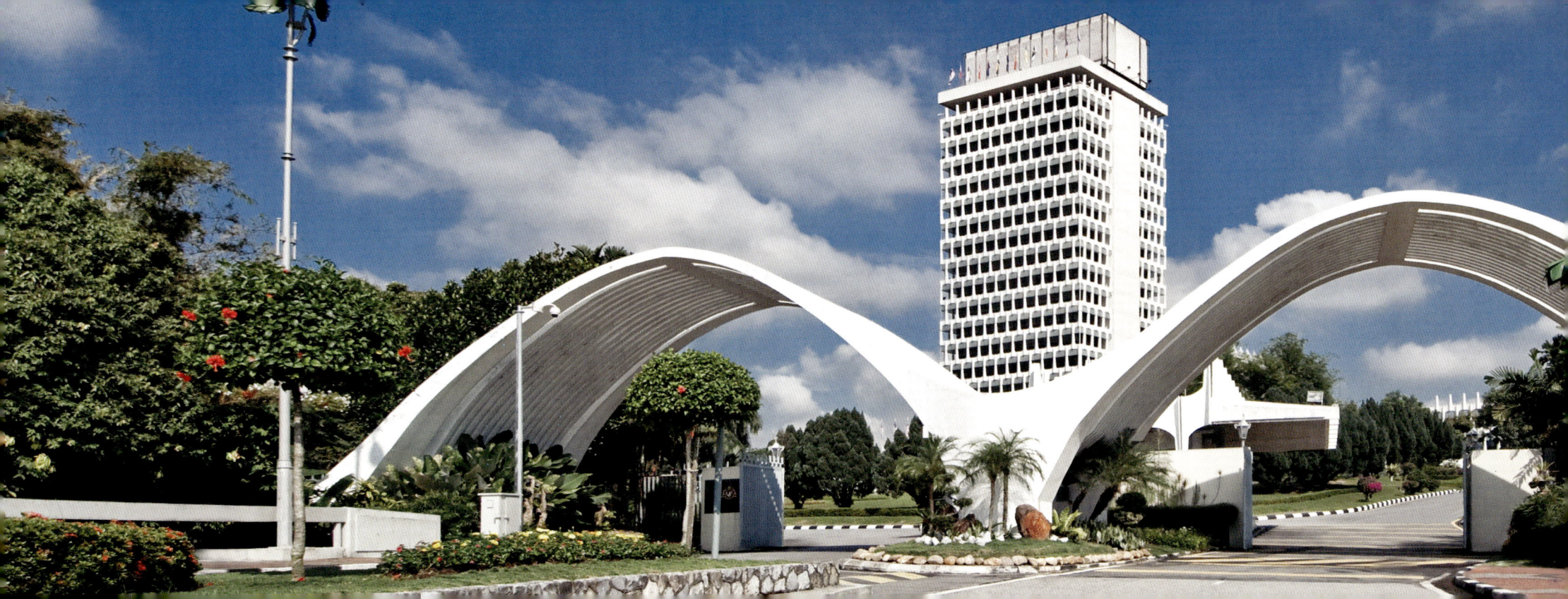

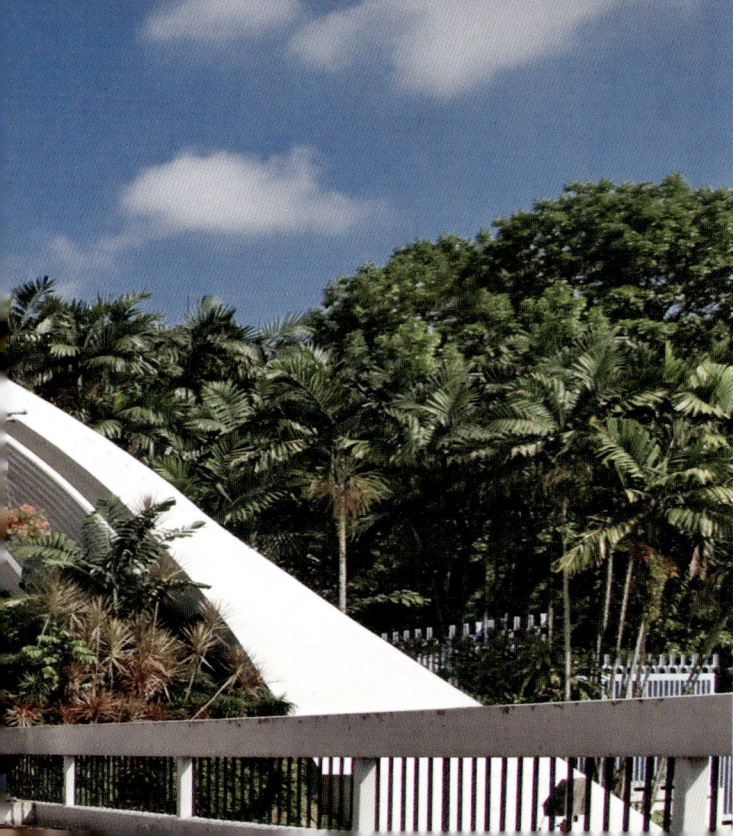
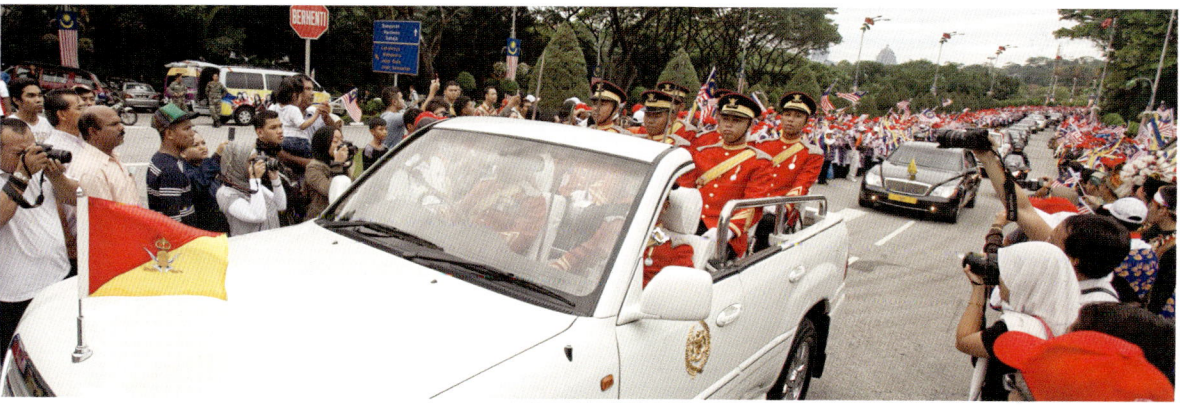

PAGES 26–27 View of the city at sunrise from Lookout Point on Ampang Hill.
PAGES 28–29 The contrasting daylight and dusk colours of the city looking east from Scott Sentral Service Suites in Brickfields.
THIS PAGE National Day celebrations along Jalan Parlimen. OPPOSITE Parliament House has hosted many contentious verbal clashes and walkouts, although chair-throwing has so far been avoided. The general elections of 2008 have, for the first time, ensured that elected MPs from the Opposition take up more than a third of the Dewan Rakyat ('Hall of the People'). Proceedings have been held in this building since November 1963, two months after the formation of Malaysia, even though the administrative capital is now the city of Putrajaya.

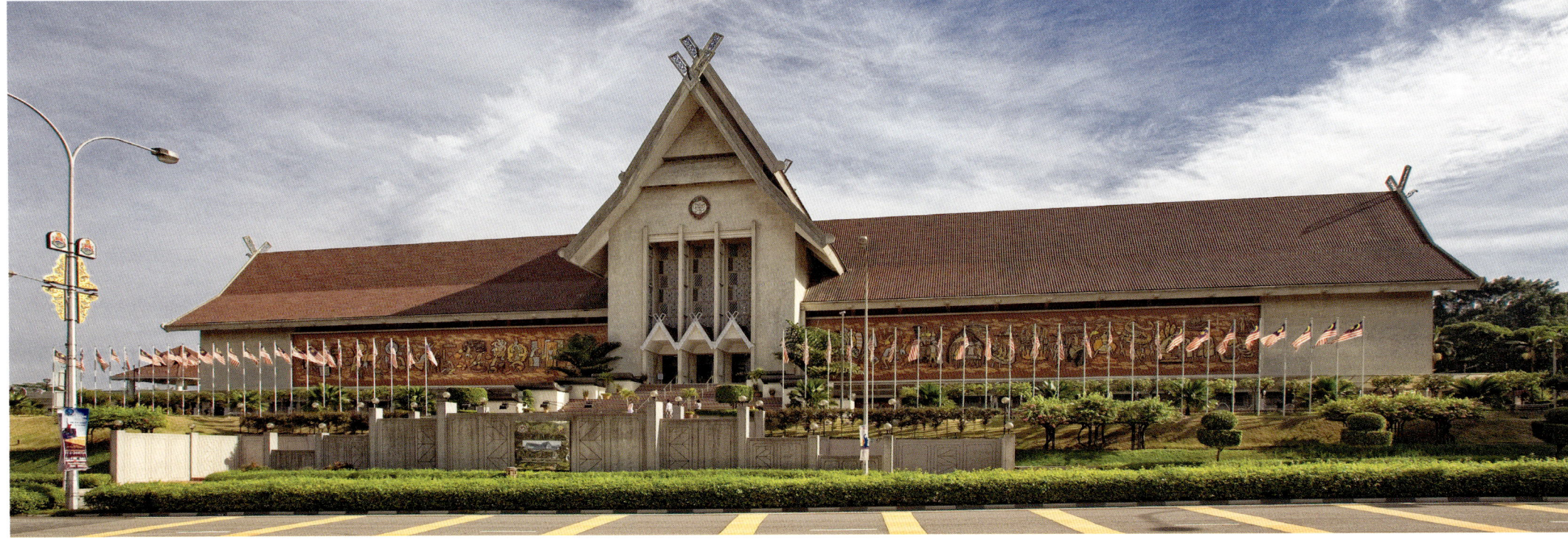

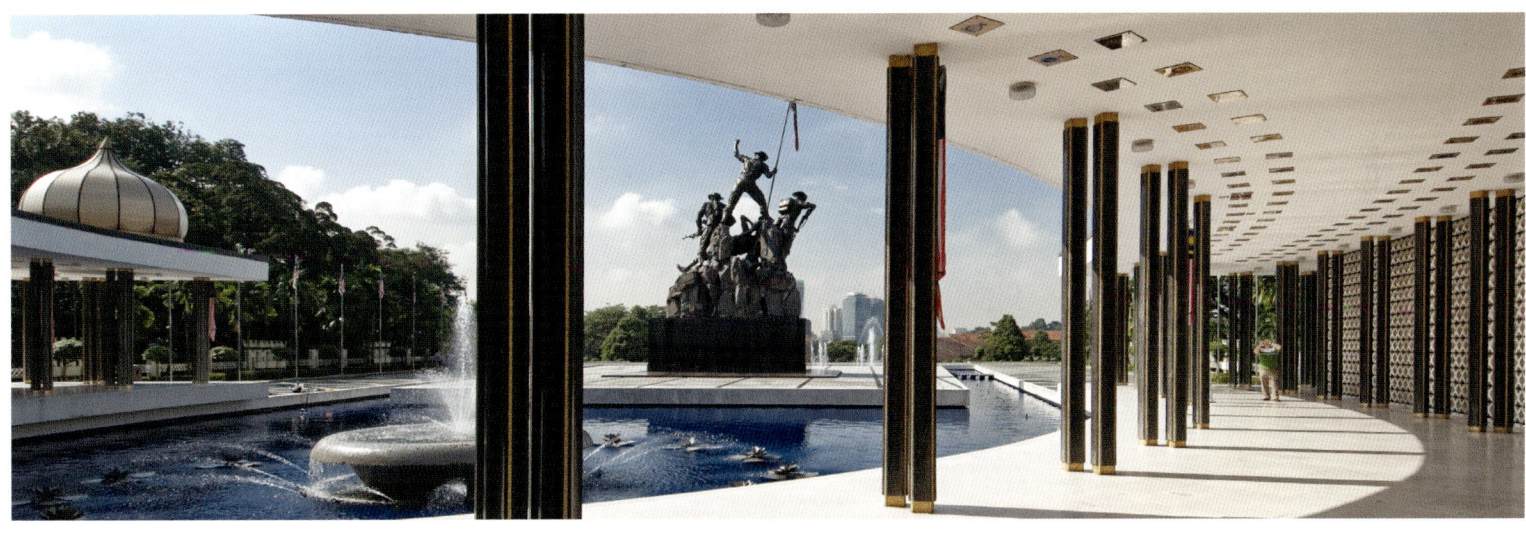

THIS PAGE Tugu Peringatan Negara (the National Monument) was built after the first Prime Minister, Tunku Abdul Rahman, was impressed by the Iwo Jiwa sculpture he saw during a trip to Washington D.C. He hired the same sculptor. The bronze monument, meant to commemorate soldiers who fell during the anti-Communist war of 1948–60 (which is euphemistically dubbed the 'Emergency'), arrived by ship in 1965. A common criticism then was that the soldiers look 'too Caucasian' rather than local. OPPOSITE The National Museum, which has hosted idiosyncratic exhibitions, with the 2002 one on ghosts breaking the attendance record.

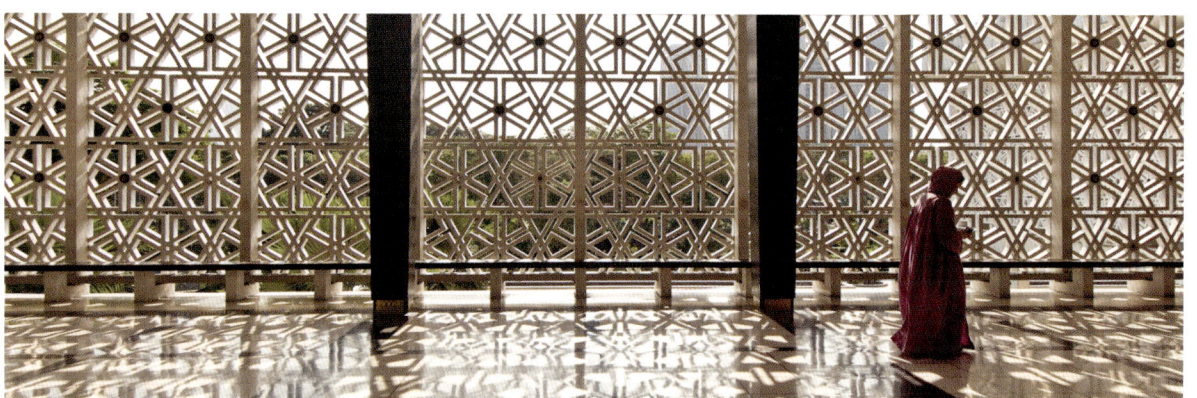
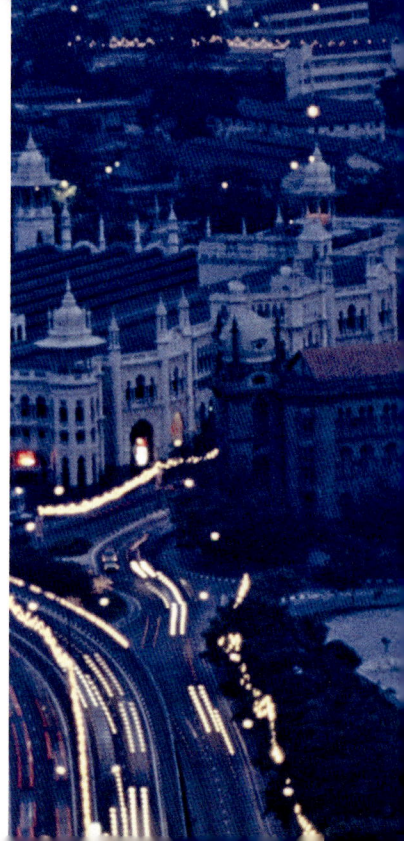

THIS PAGE AND OPPOSITE Masjid Negara (The National Mosque), completed in 1965, continues to be popular for congregations, especially on Friday. Unlike most mosques built since, it eschews overt Arabian architectural influence. The main dome (stylised to resemble a fan rather than an onion bulb), was originally grey but was replaced with blue tiles in the late 1980s due to staining.

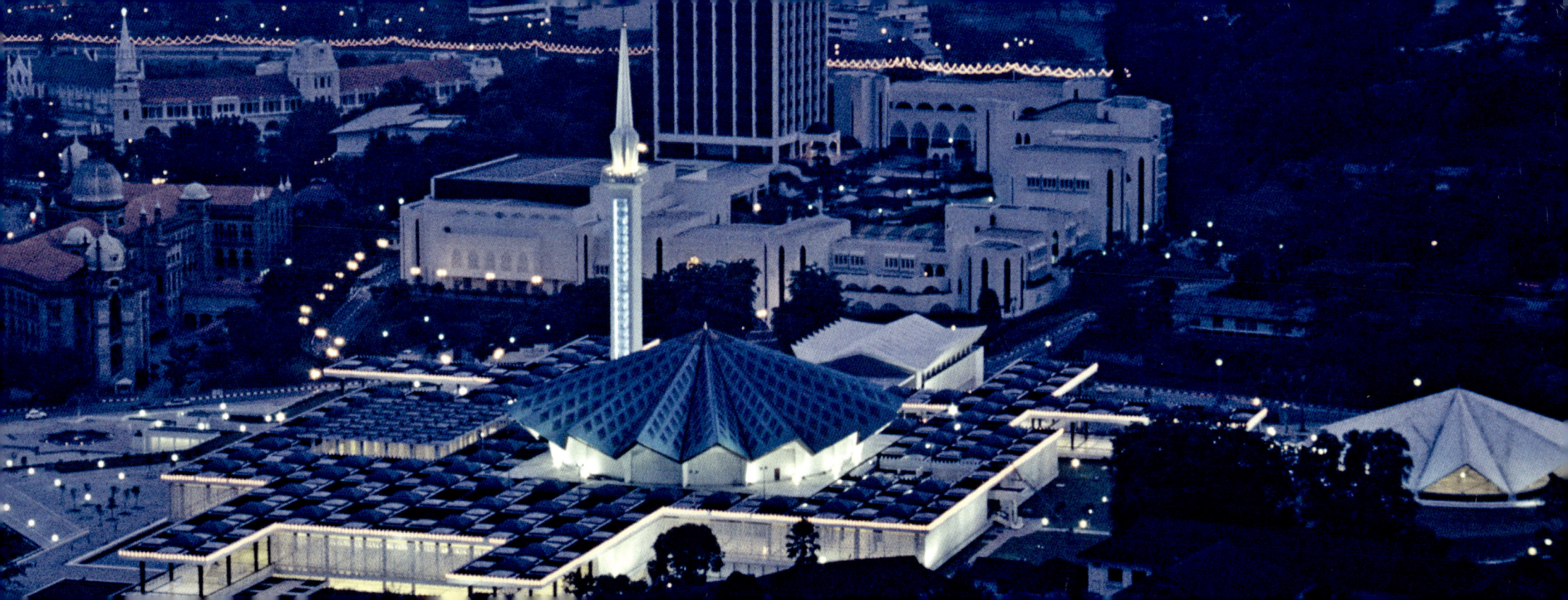

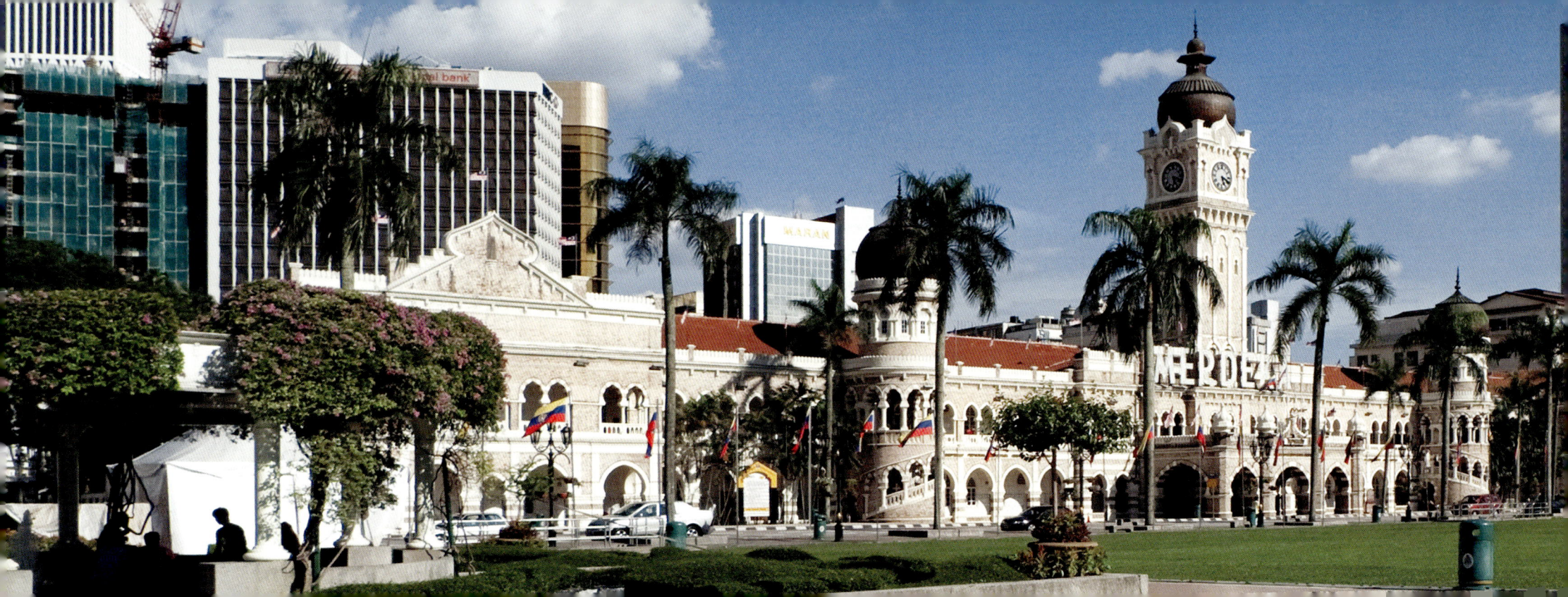

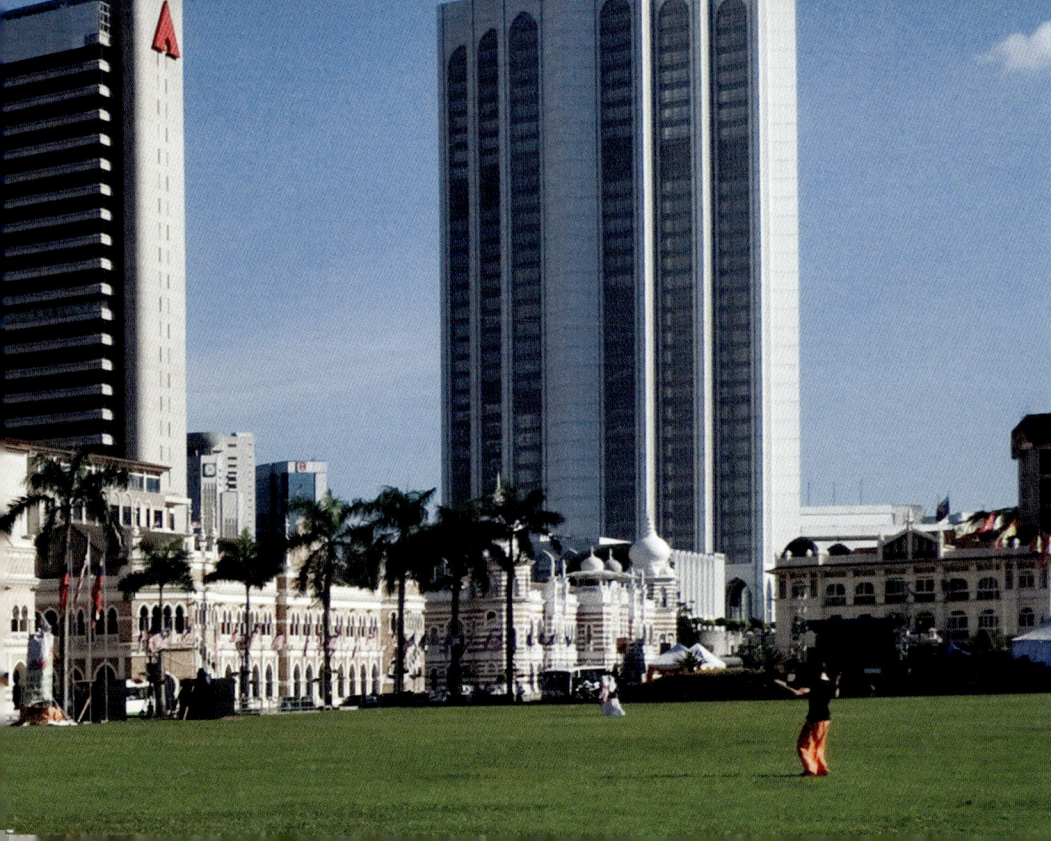

THIS PAGE The Sultan Abdul Samad Building, the dominant postcard image of KL before the Petronas Twin Towers were built. Opened in 1897, its unconventional Moorish-inspired architecture continues to be a thing of beauty. The white tower on the right is Dayabumi, built during the go-getting 1980s as a commercial centre; it later became the headquarters for national petroleum corporation Petronas before the construction of the Twin Towers.

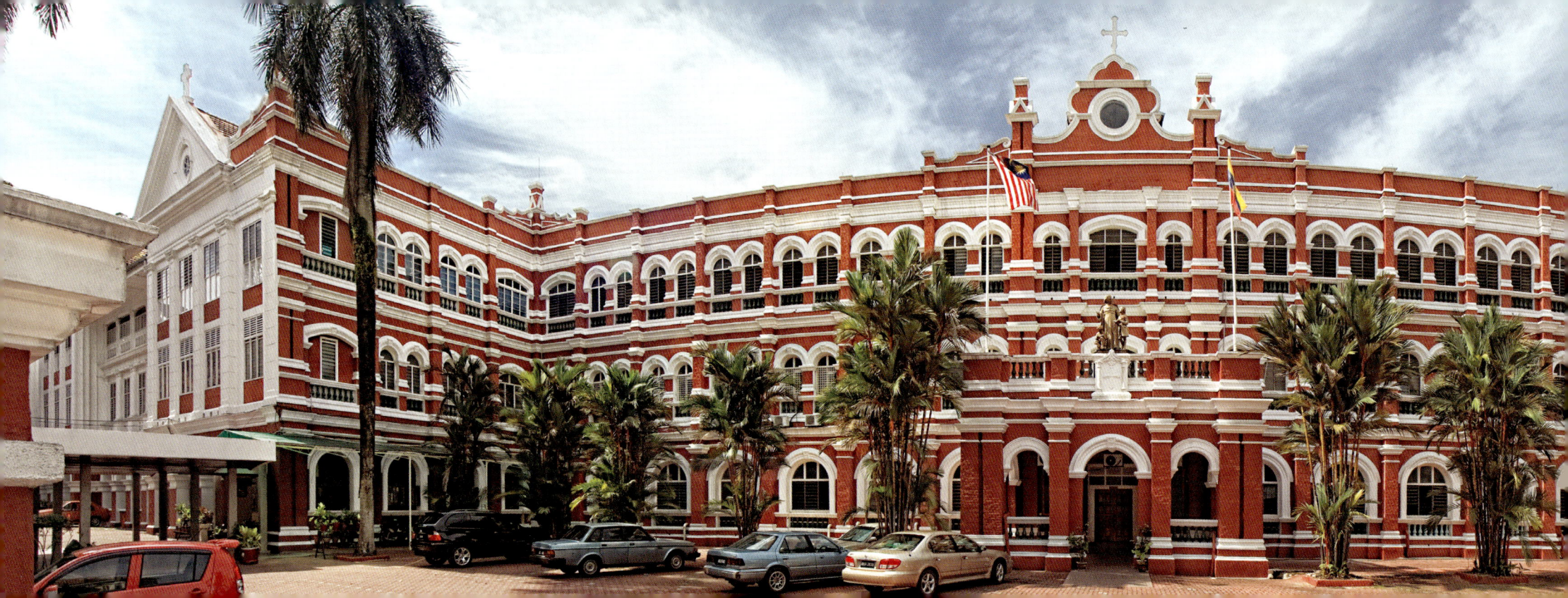

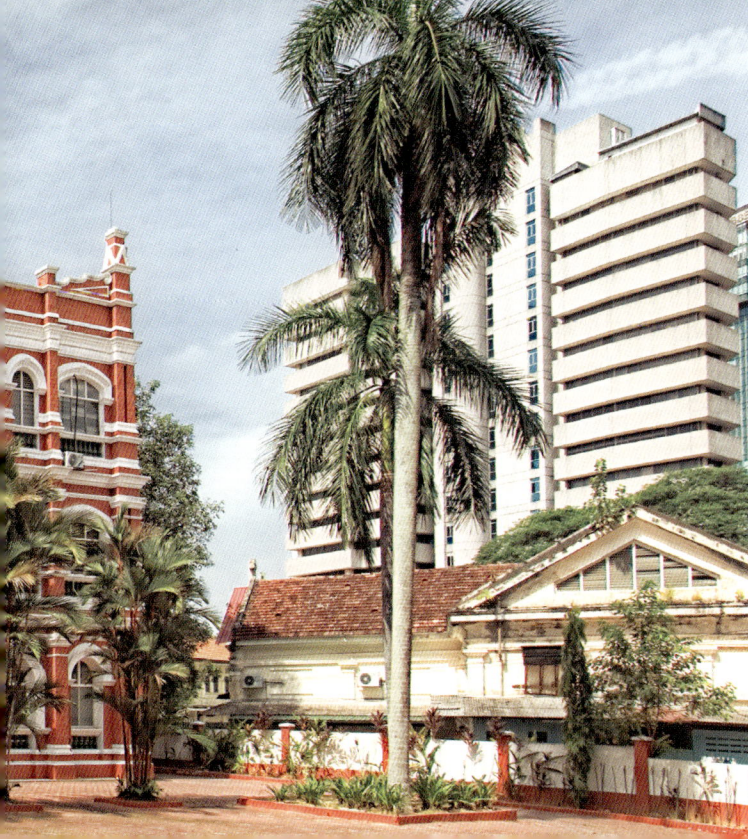

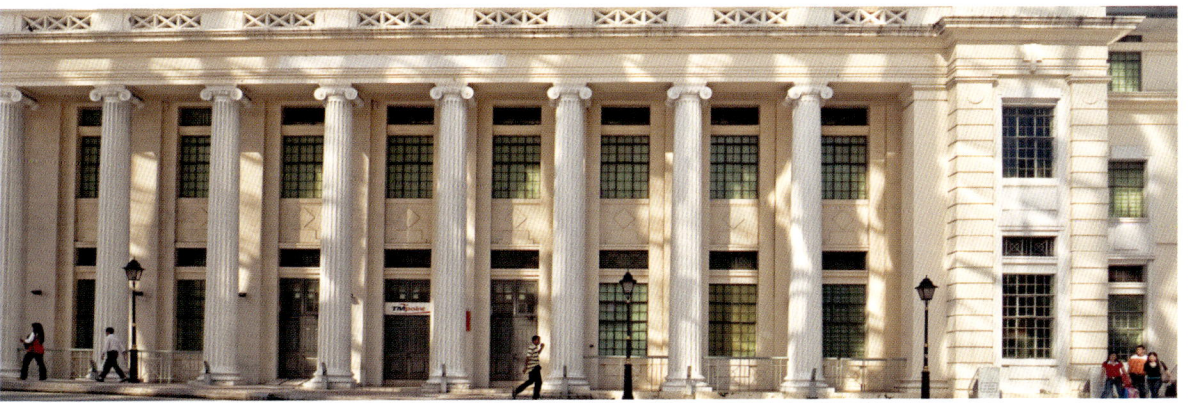

THIS PAGE The neo-classical façade of the Telekom Museum on Jalan Gereja. OPPOSITE St John's Institution, one of the oldest boys' schools in KL, was established in 1904. Started by missionaries, it now follows the national syllabus. As with most Malaysian schools set up by the British, students still take pride in certain decades-old rituals.

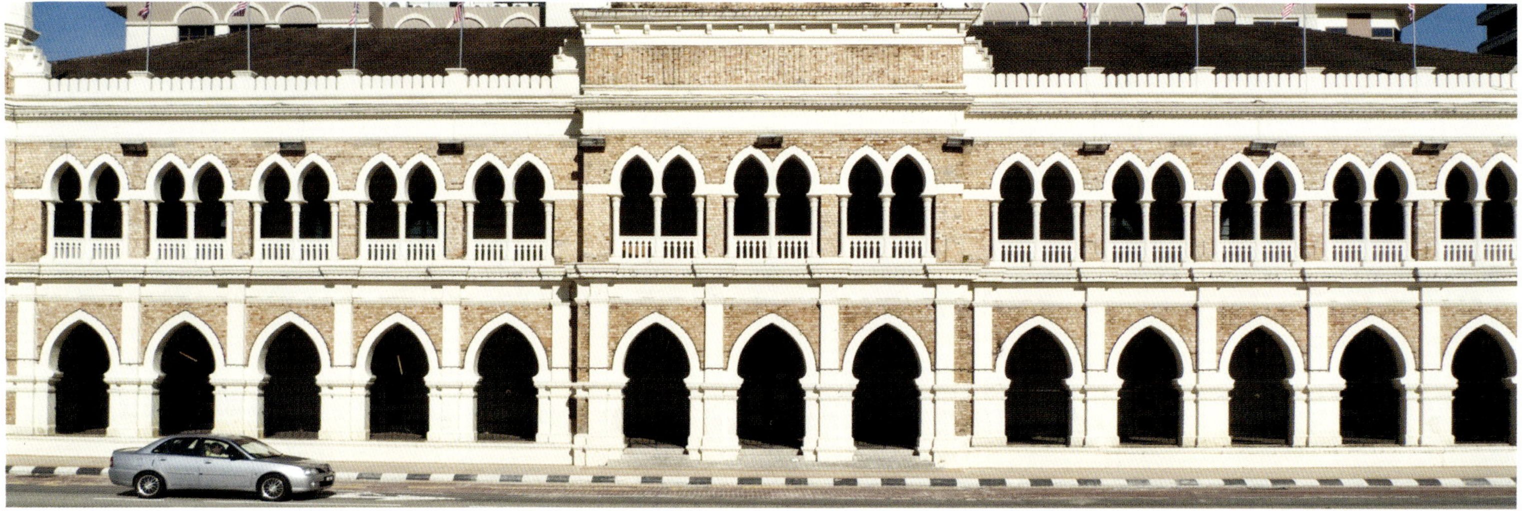

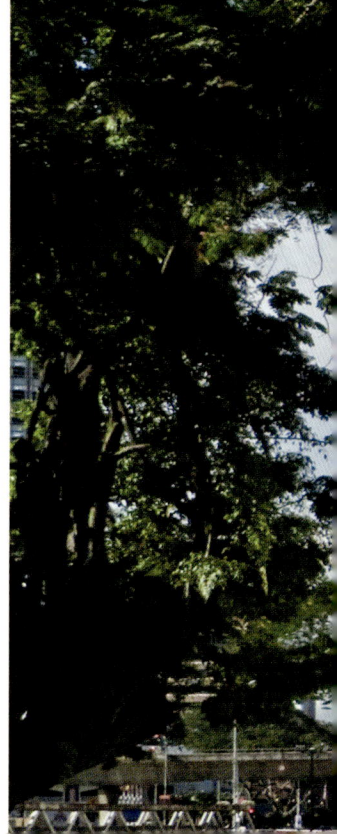

THIS PAGE AND OPPOSITE The Moorish-inspired buildings in the old heart of the British colonial administration around what is now Dataran Merdeka (formerly 'The Padang' or field) were constructed in the late 19th and early 20th centuries. Credit for their design goes not to the architect A.C. Norman but to C.E. Spooner, director of the Public Works Department, who had served previously in Ceylon (now Sri Lanka).

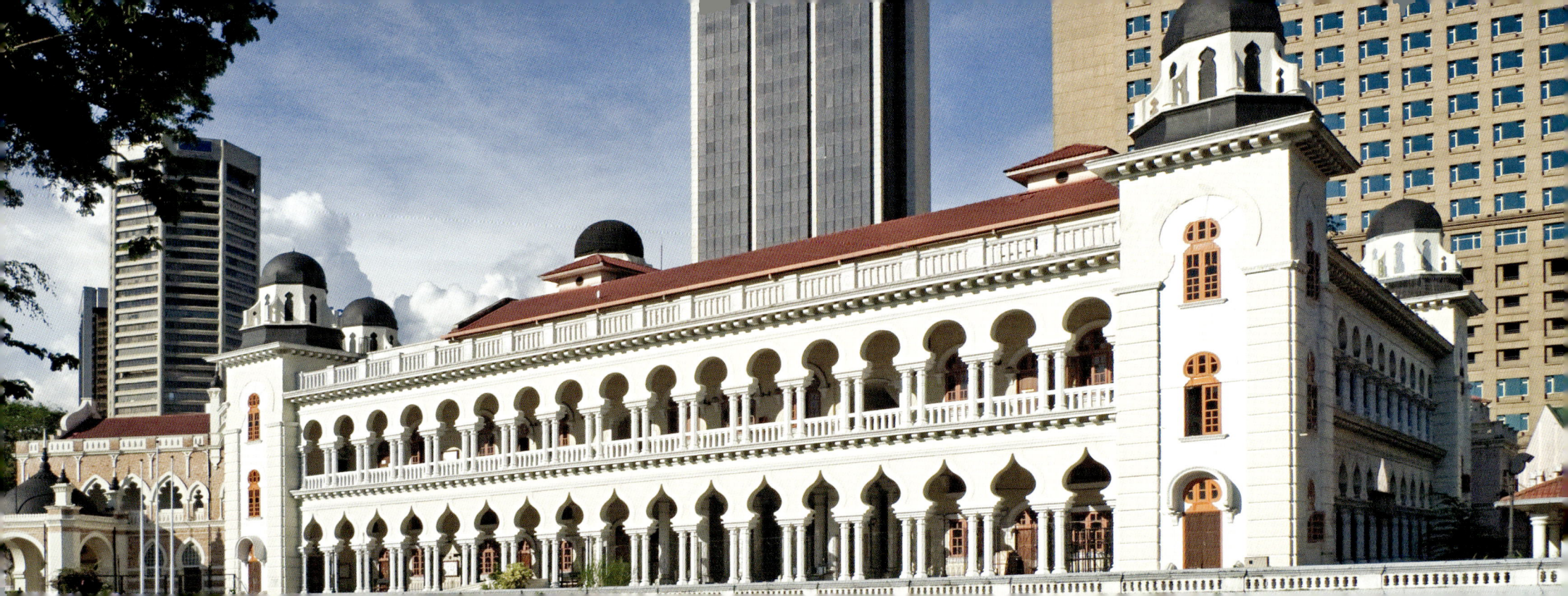

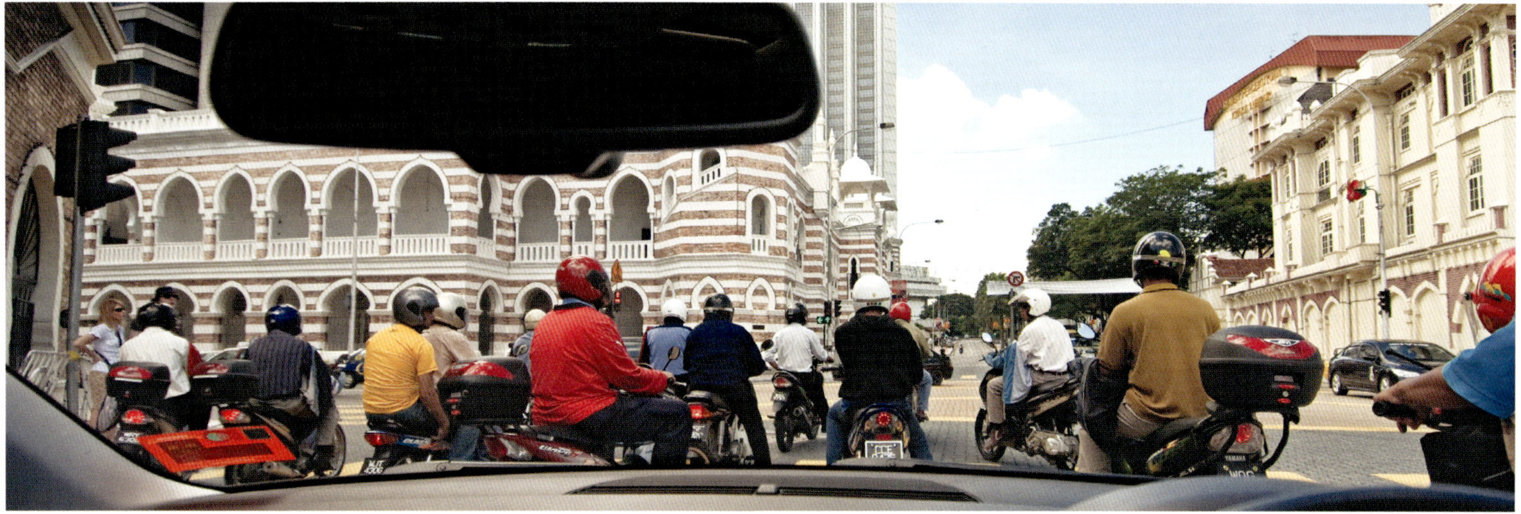

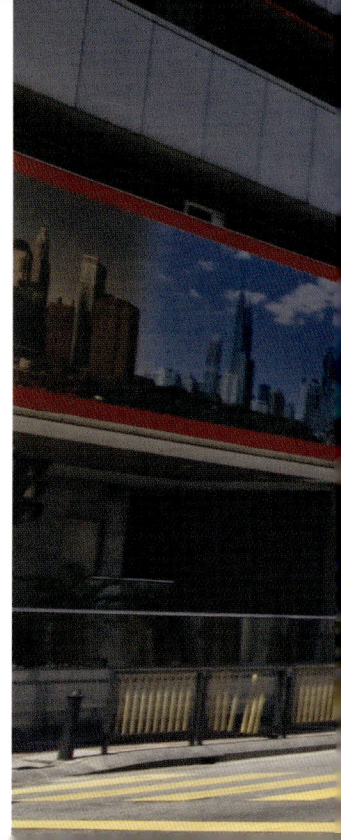

THIS PAGE Bikers waiting for the lights change next to Dataran Merdeka. Although these are well-behaved ones, the area is notorious for nocturnal *mat rempit* (illegal bike racers).
OPPOSITE Medan Pasar, formerly Market Square.

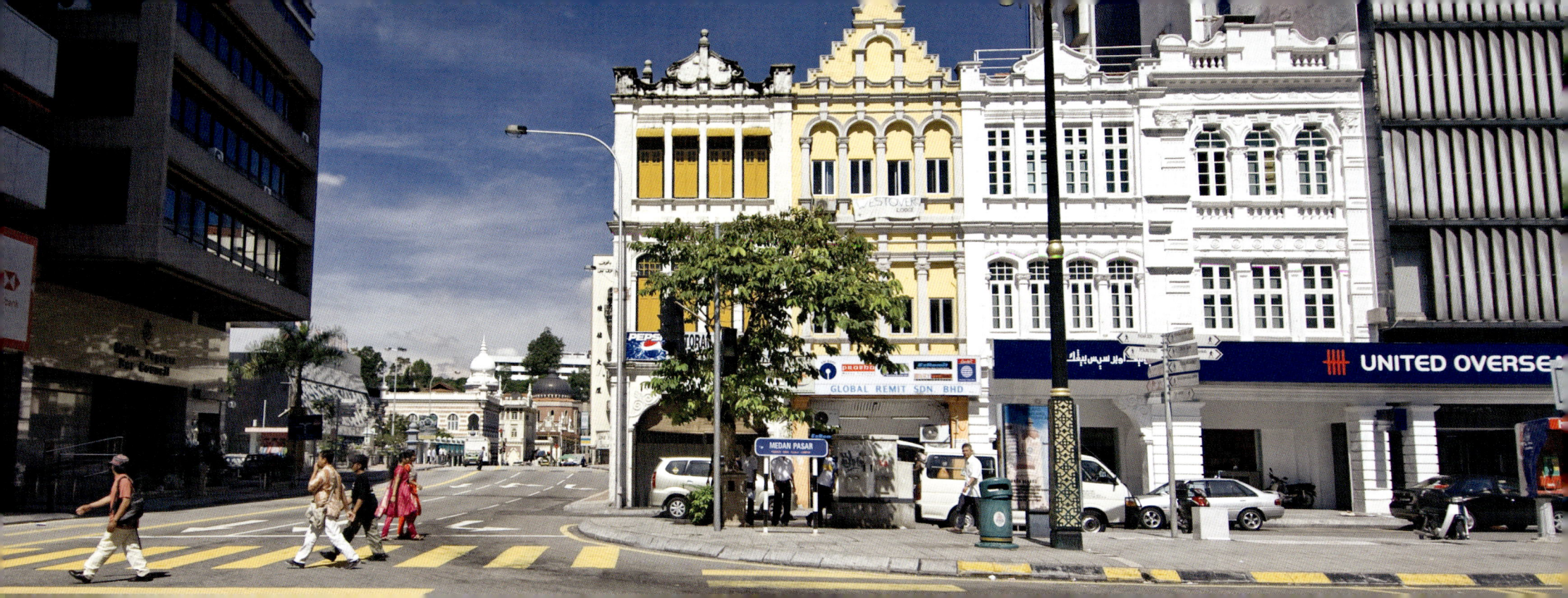

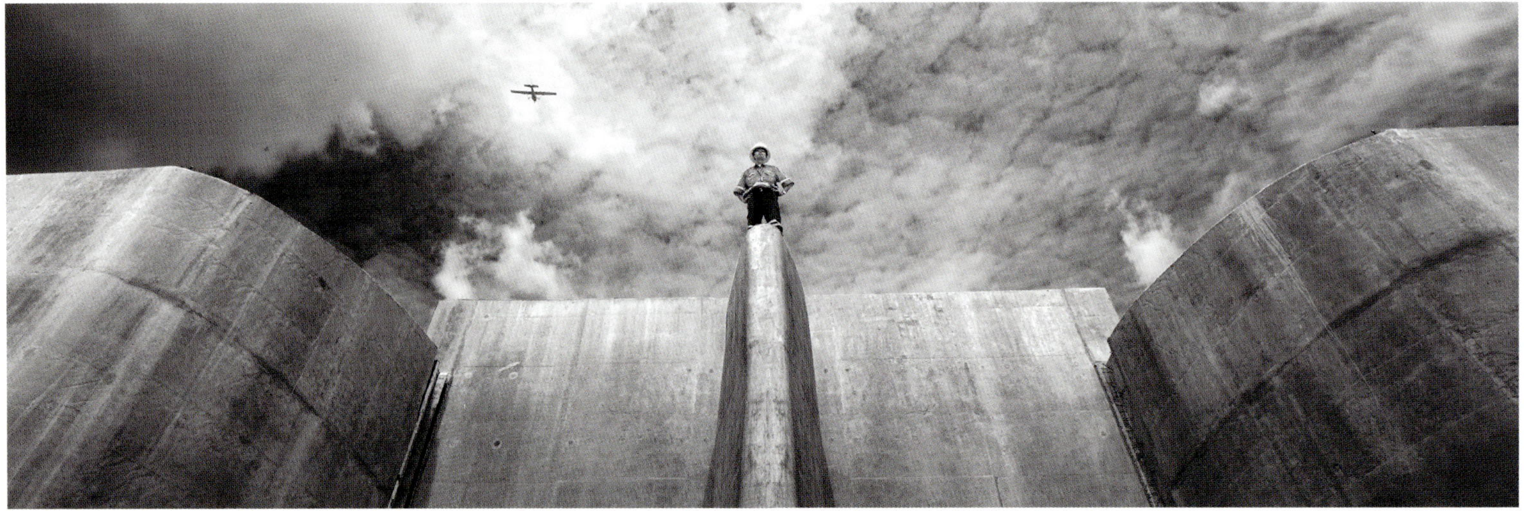

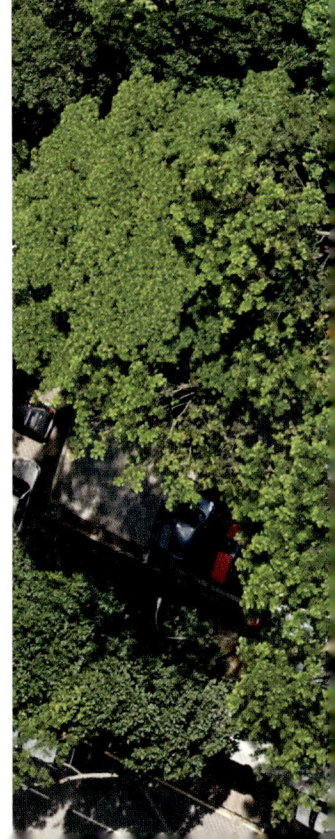

THIS PAGE Worker inspecting the soon-to-be-completed flood water holding pond at Taman Desa lake, part of the SMART tunnel scheme completed in 2007. The scheme consists of a stormwater tunnel to reduce the impact of KL's frequent flash floods and—by incorporating a motorway inside the tunnel—to ease traffic congestion. However, floods still bring roads to a standstill. OPPOSITE The road leading to KL Tower.

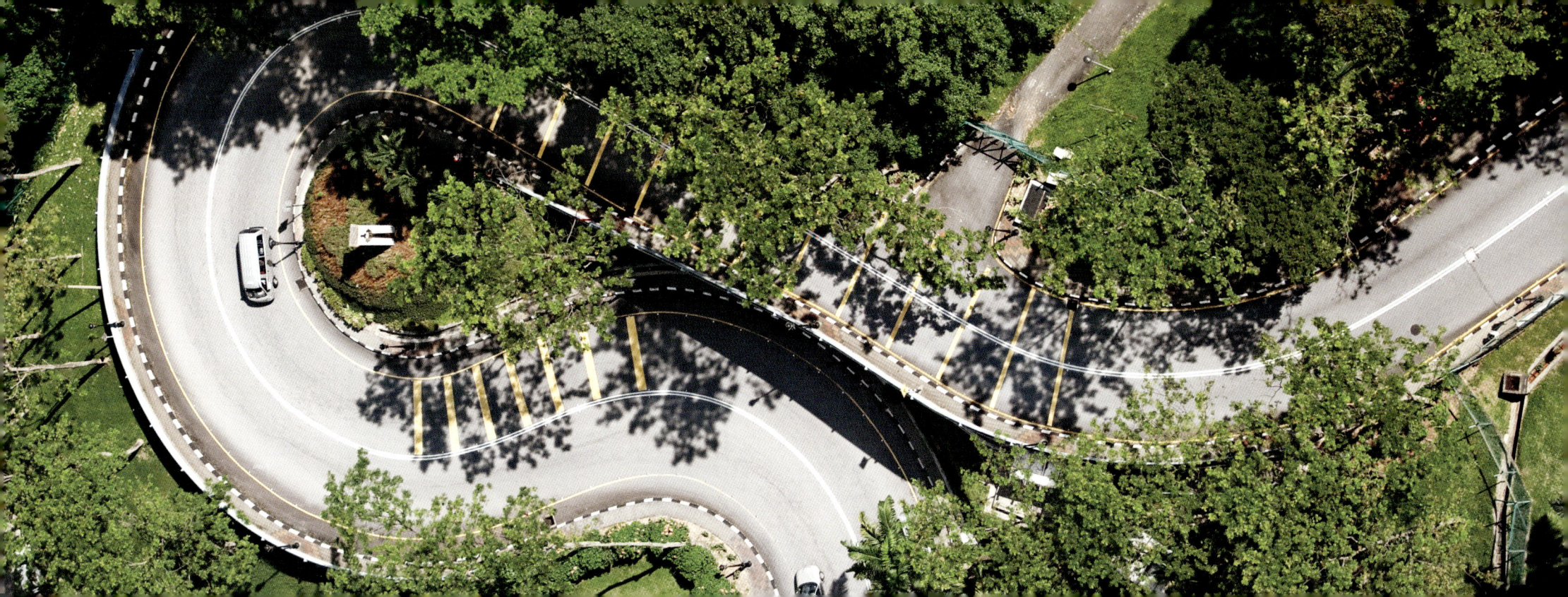

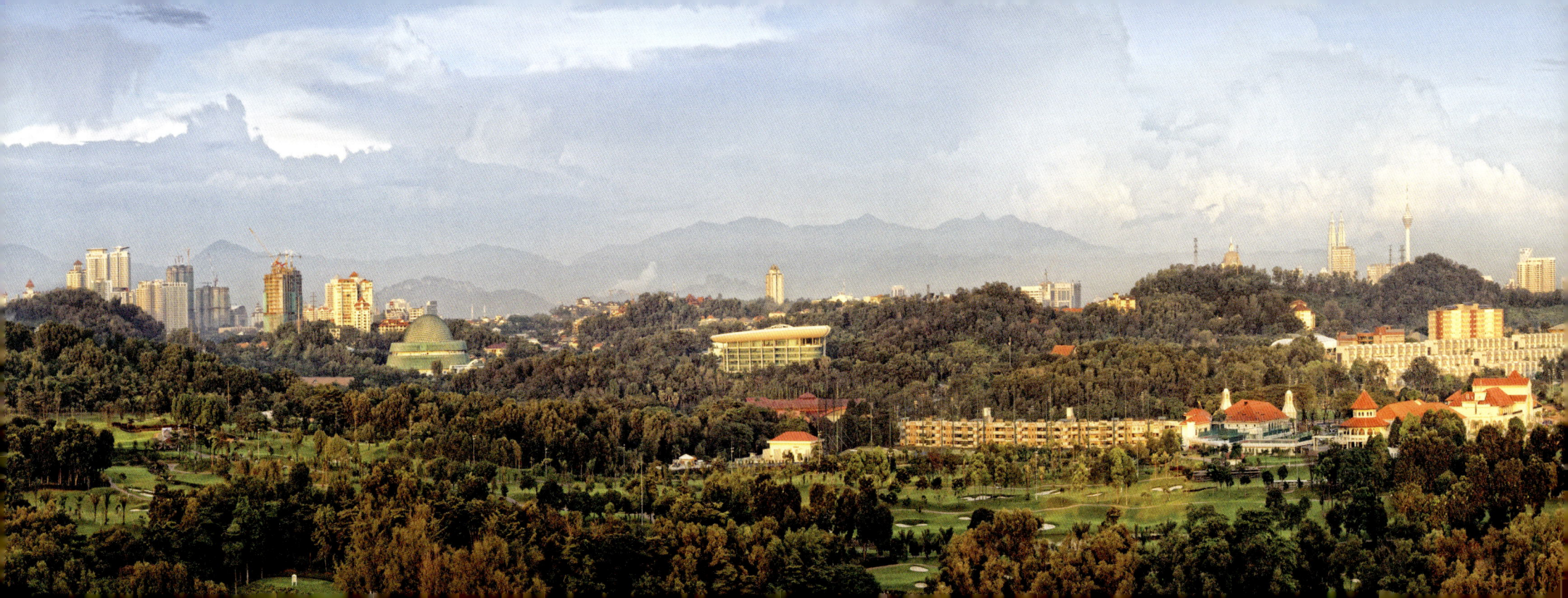

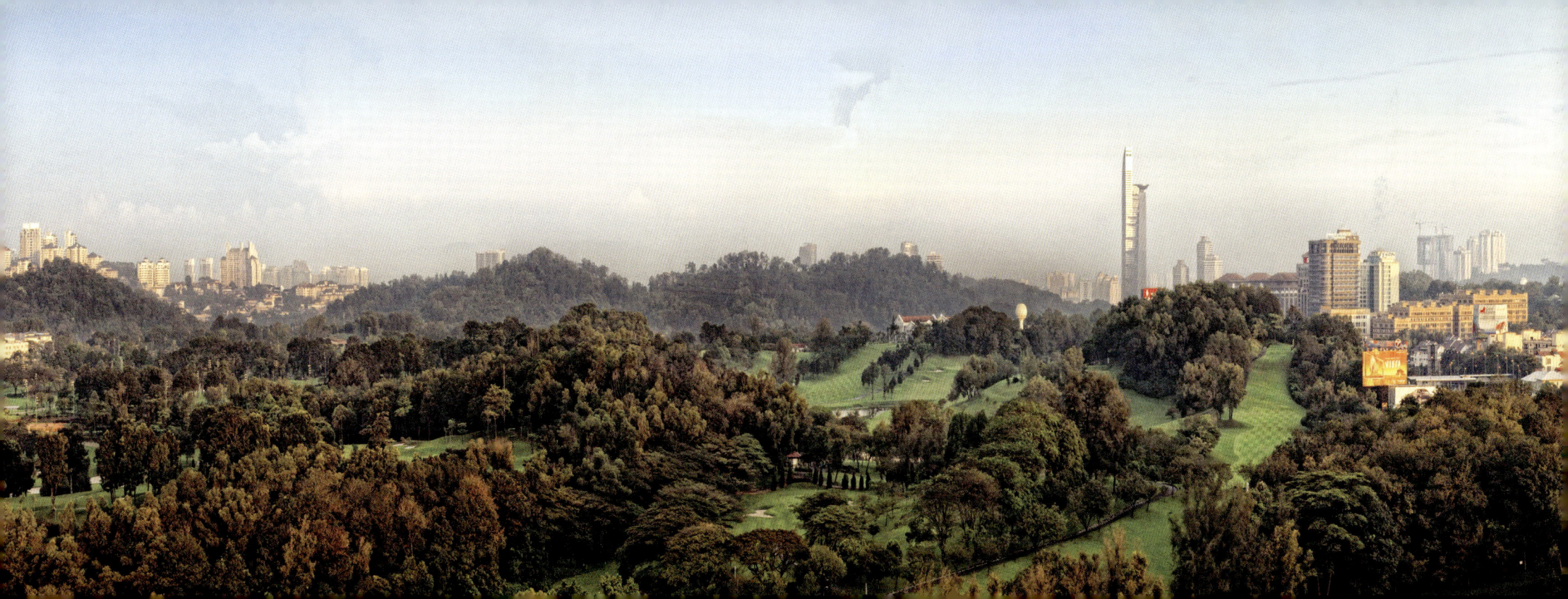

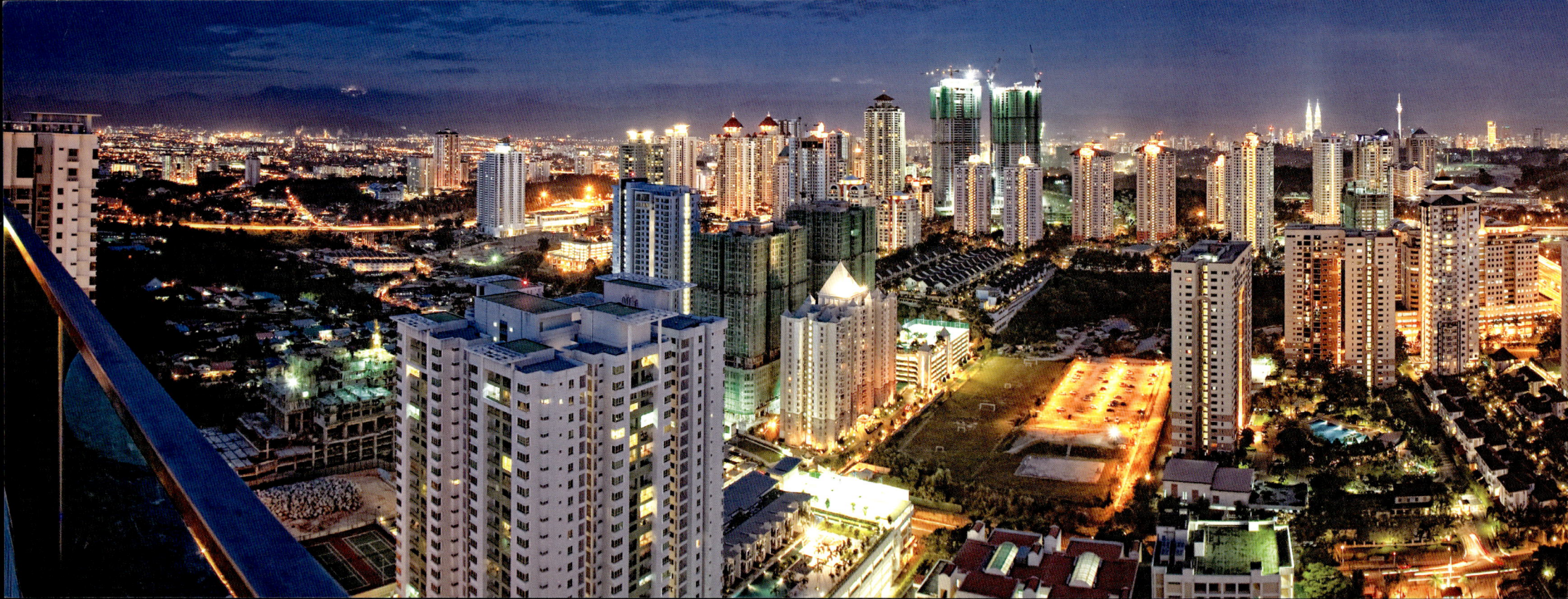

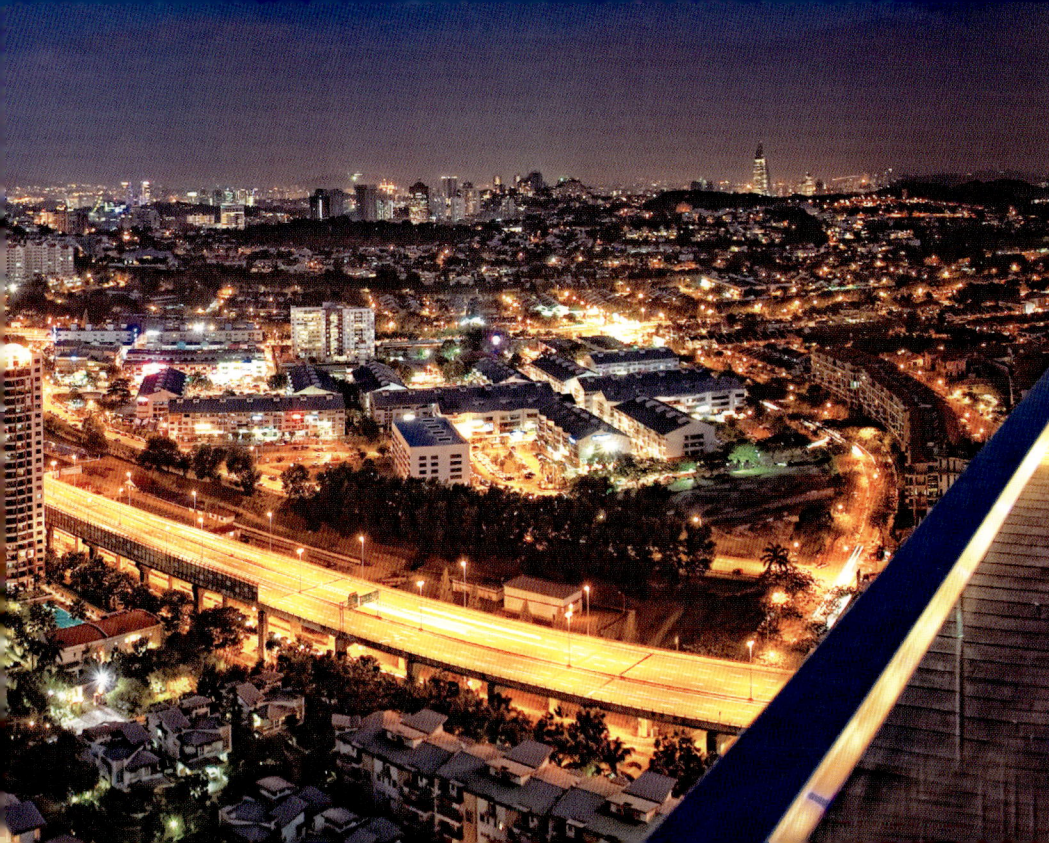

PAGES 46–47 Panoramic view of the city from Taman Tun Dr Ismail. THIS PAGE The view from across Mont Kiara towards the city centre. The Petronas Twin Towers and KL Tower are visible in the distance, as are the mountain-top lights of Genting Highlands to the left of the photograph. The city of KL has a population of 2 million, making it one of the less crowded Asian capital cities. People really started living in high-rise flats and condominiums only in the 1980s, but there are now new ones being constructed all around.

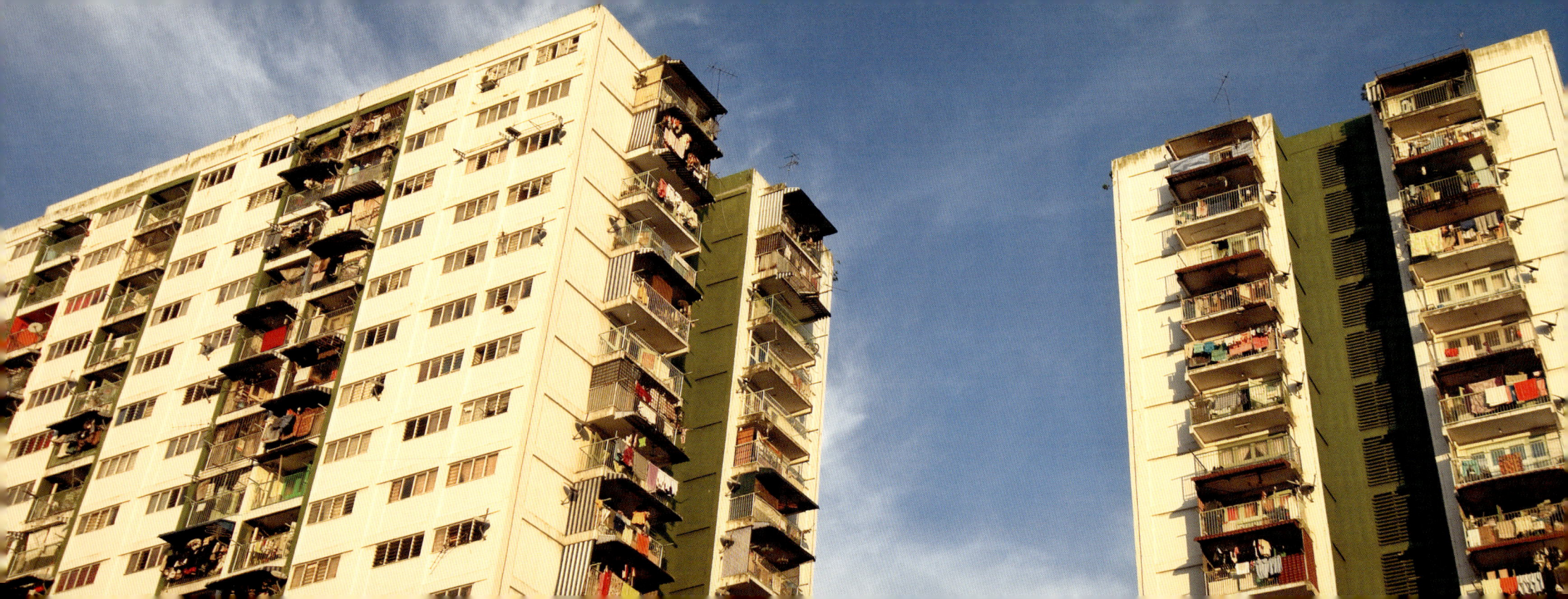

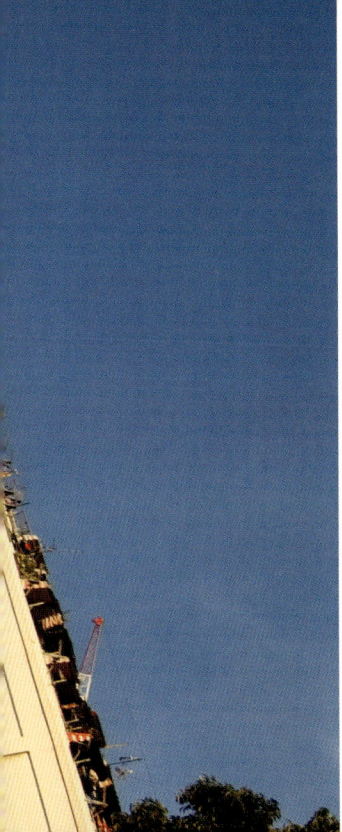

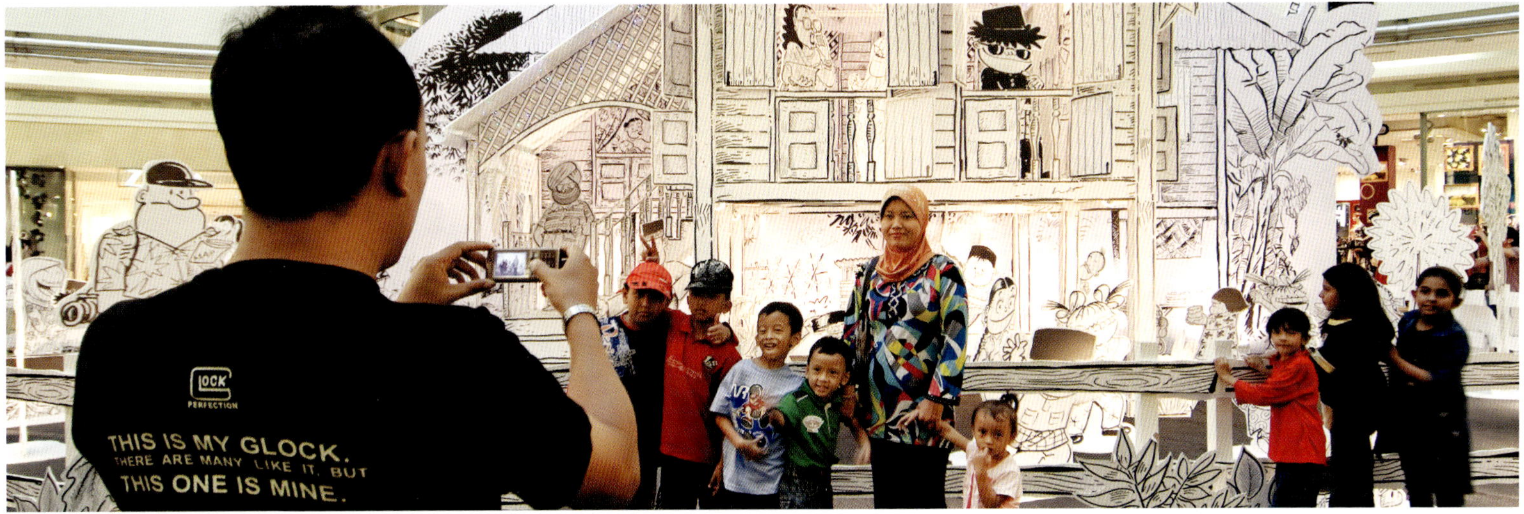

THIS PAGE A replica of kampong life, in the middle of one of KL's shopping malls. The cartoon is by Lat, Malaysia's best-known cartoonist. OPPOSITE Low-cost flats in Bangsar Utama, where memories of kampongs may also reside, but which will fade further with each generation.

THIS PAGE Kampung Baru still retains a village-like charm as the metropolis grows vertically around it.

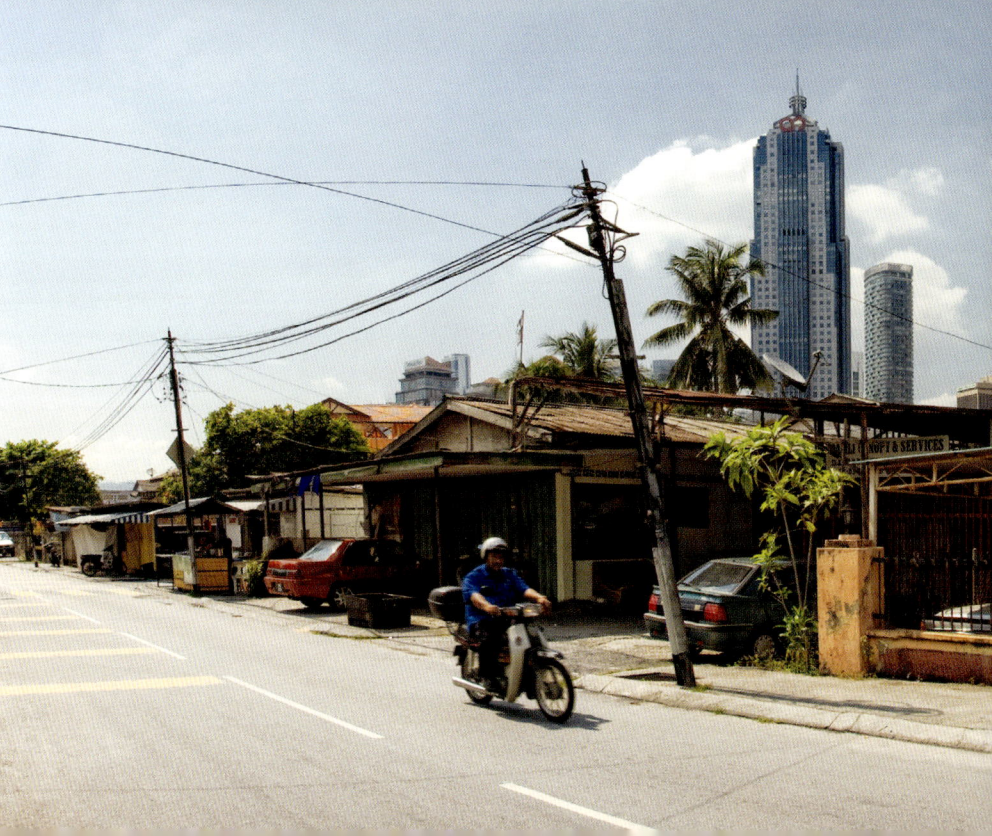

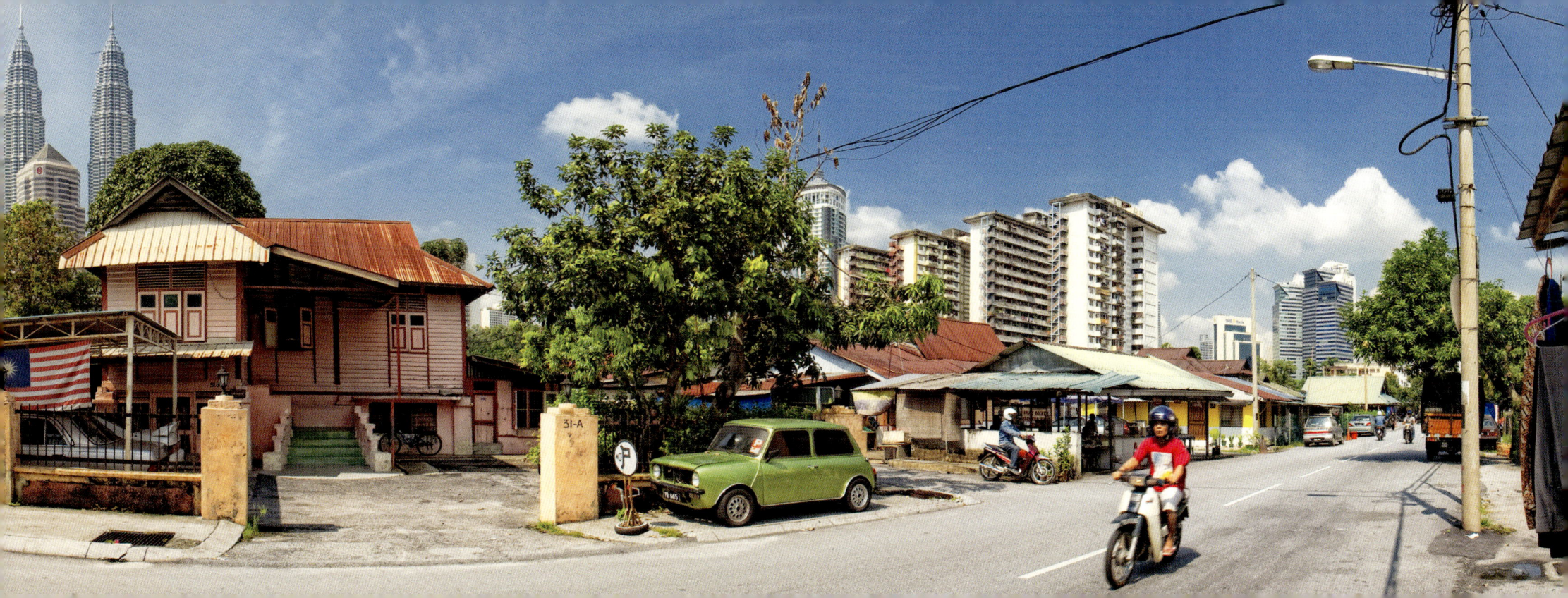

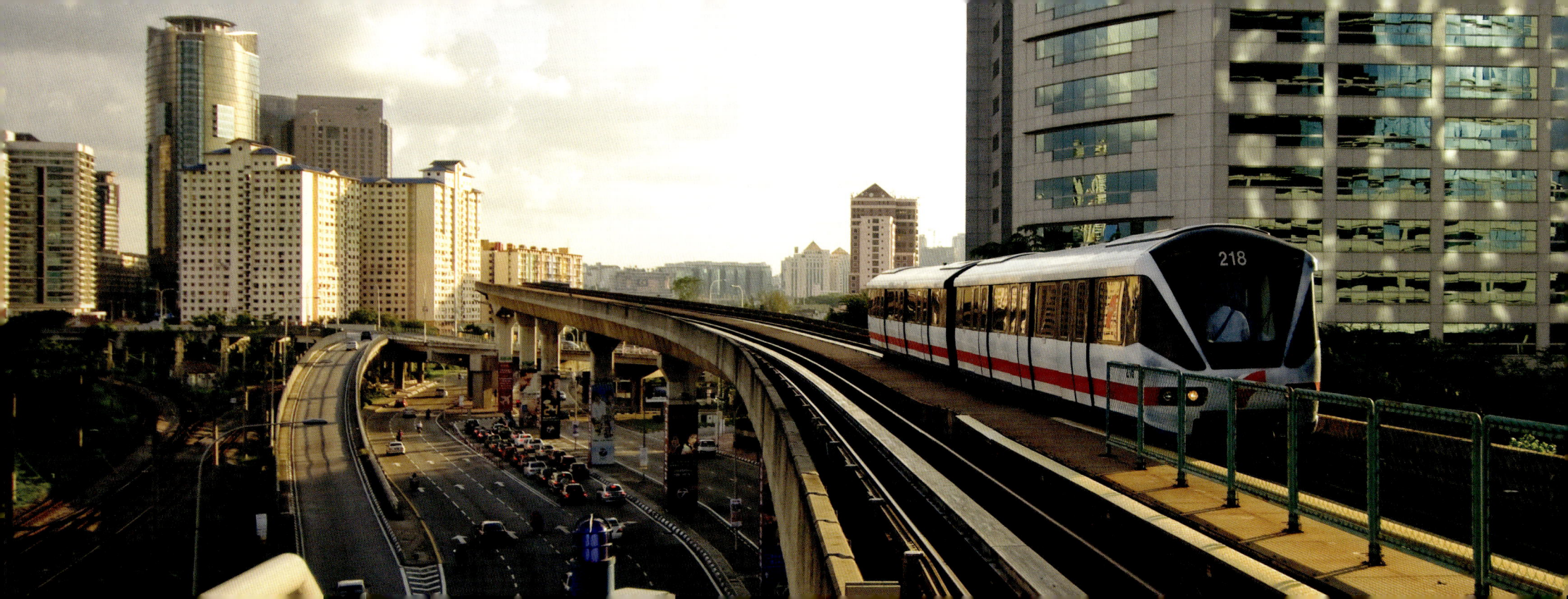

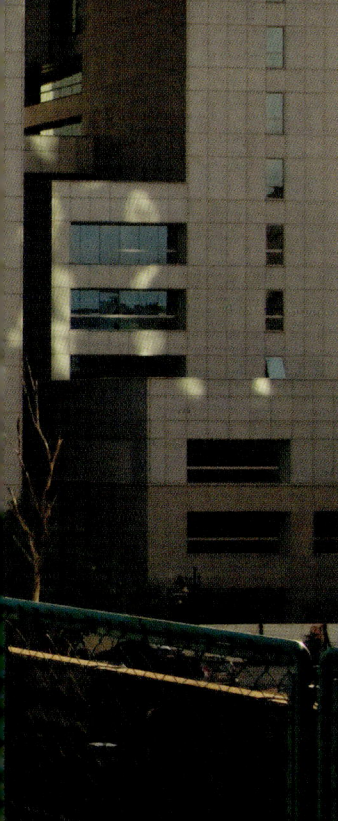

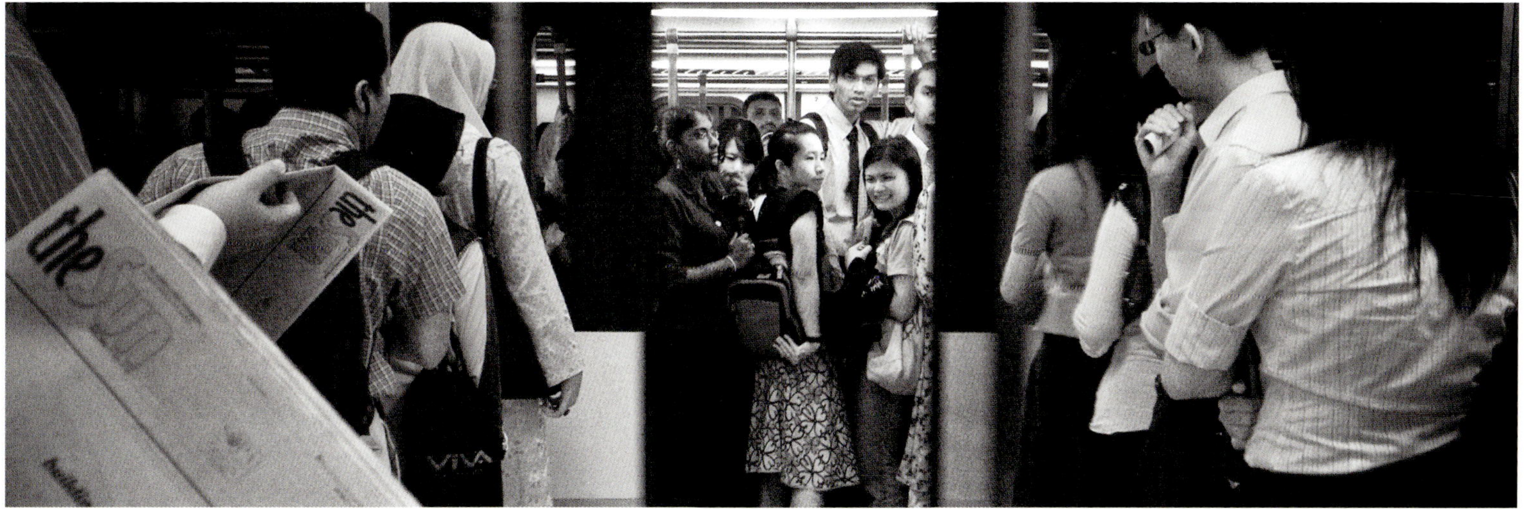

THIS PAGE AND OPPOSITE KL's urban rail system started in the mid-1990s and is constantly expanding. Over 300,000 people use it daily. The sleek single-train compartments have taken over from the previously ubiquitous, but now phased out, pink minibuses as the most iconic form of public transport. But, yes, traffic jams still occur.

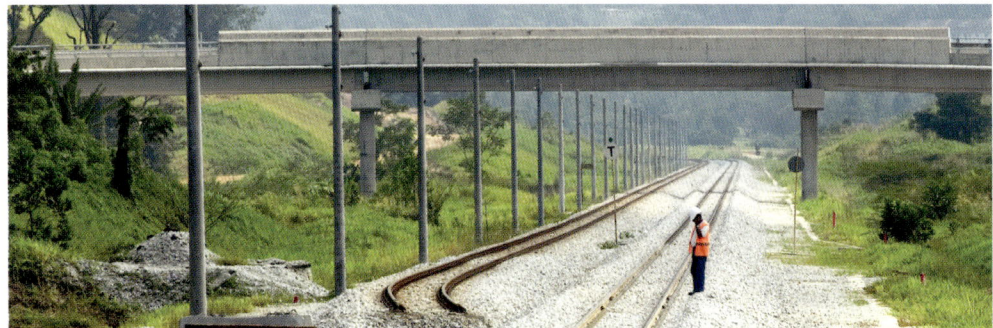

THIS PAGE Worker inspecing railway lines near Kuala Lumpur. OPPOSITE The E & O Express, an incongruously luxurious mode of travel, and hence strictly for tourists. It's stopping at the old KL Railway Station, although other trains bypass this century-old building in favour of the newer KL Sentral.

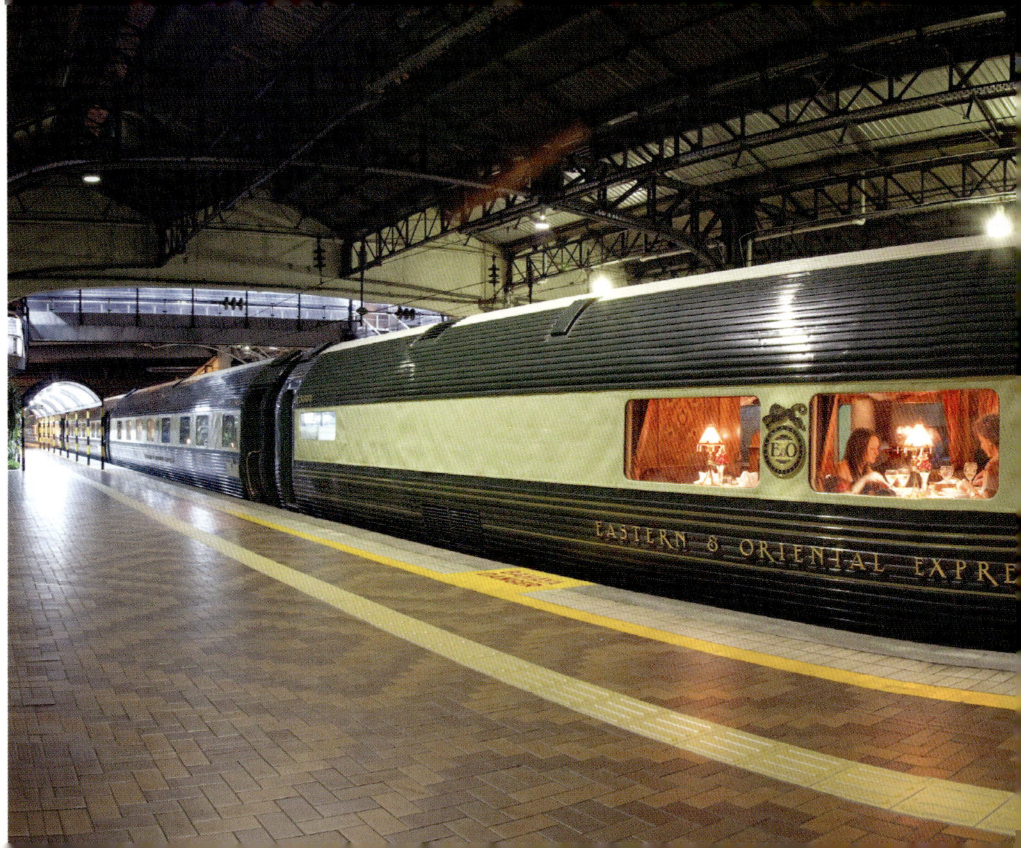

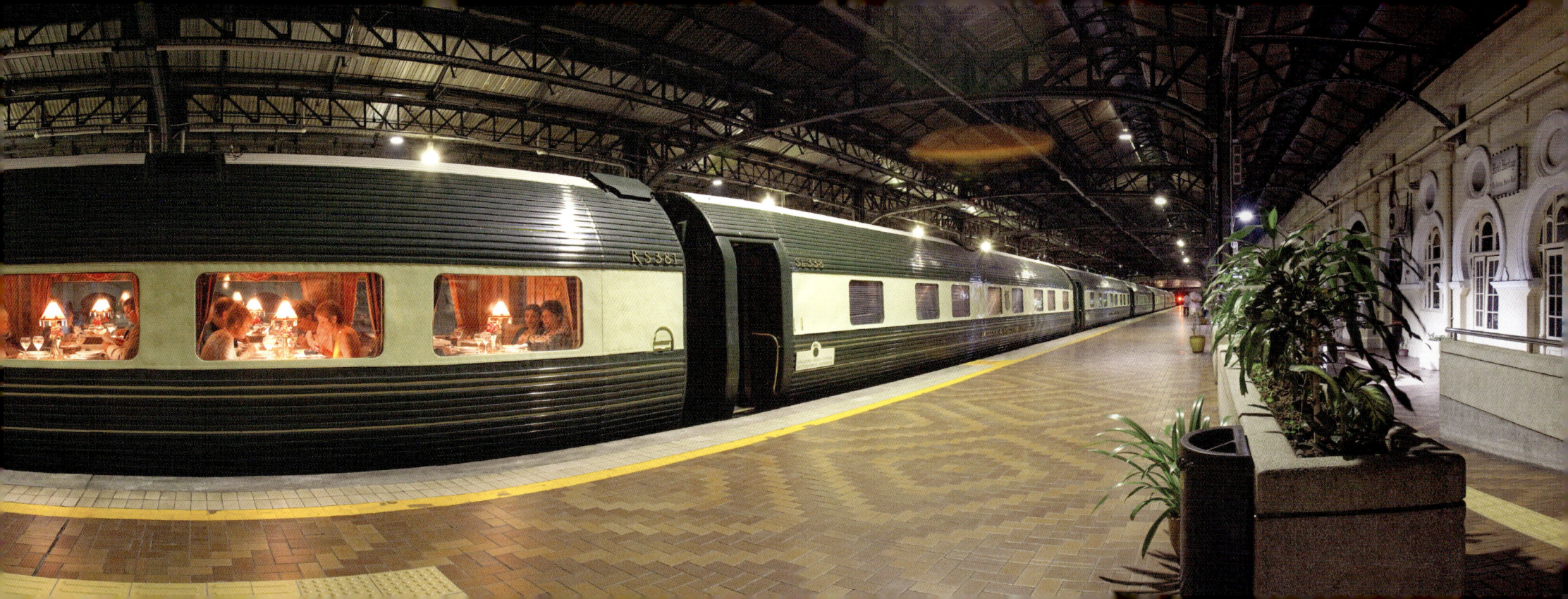

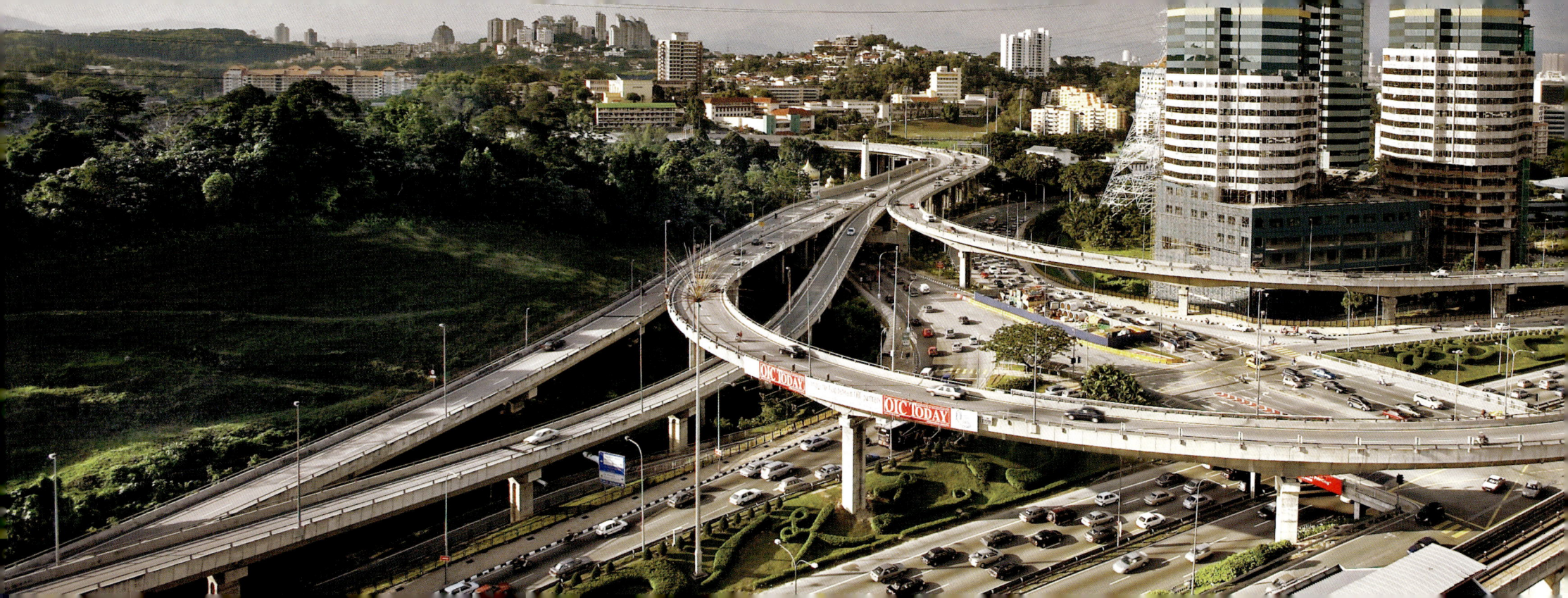

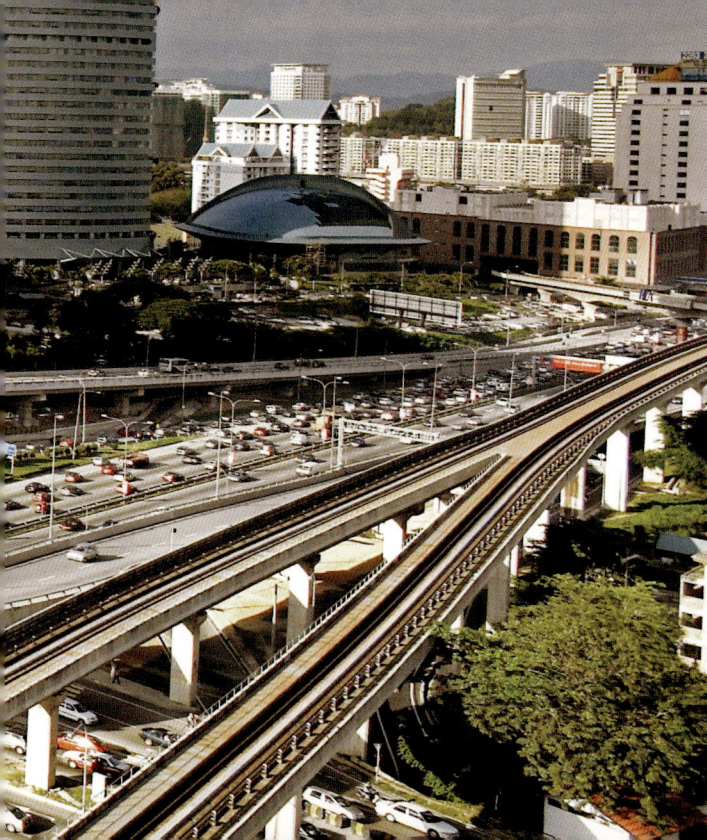

THIS PAGE The Federal Highway, the elevated Kerinchi Link and Jalan Pantai Dalam converge near the Universiti LRT station. The scene prompts all sorts of cardio-vascular metaphors. The 'twin towers' here are not the KLCC towers. To their right is the base of Menara TM.

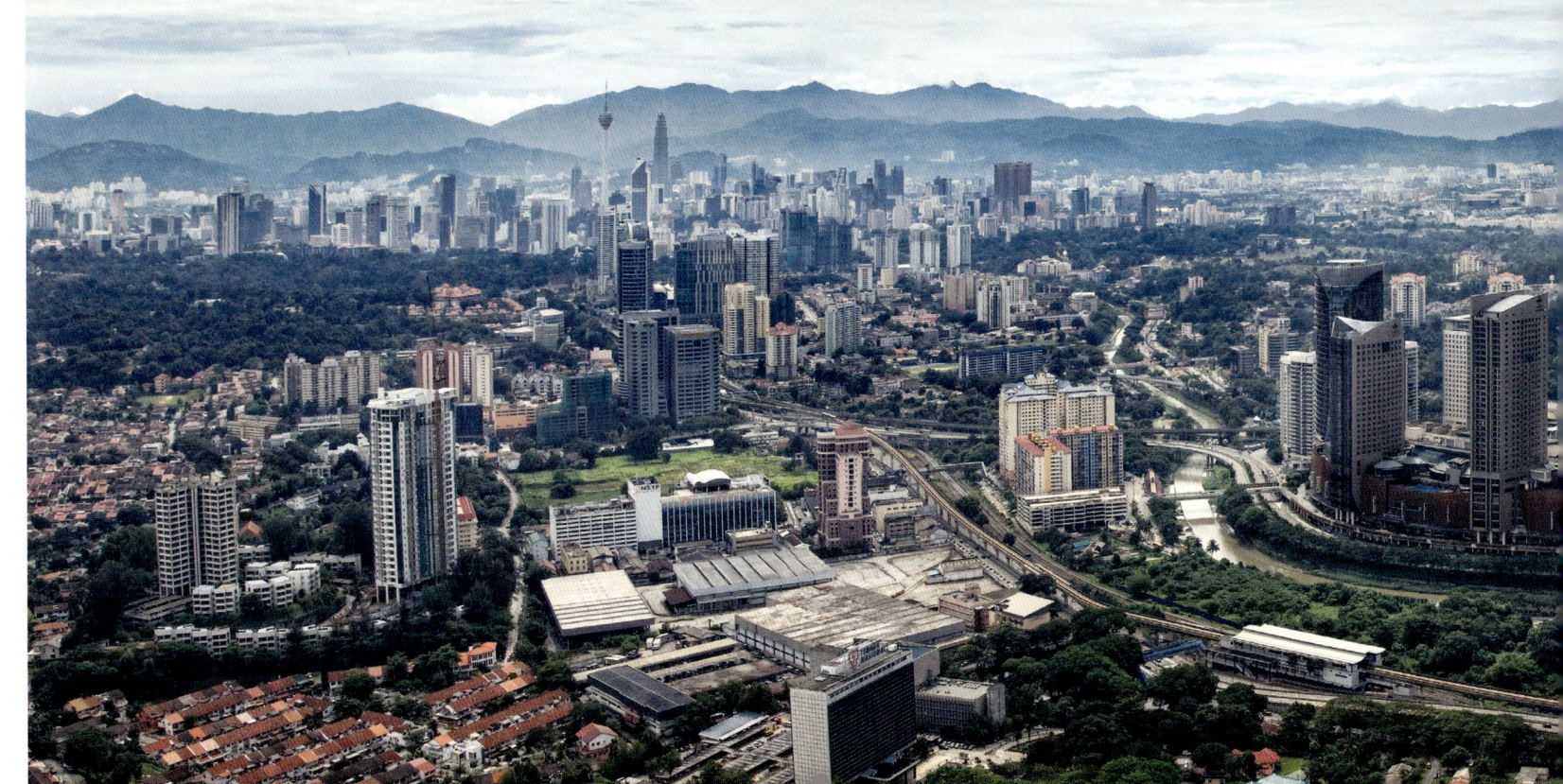

THIS PAGE The view from Menara TM towards central KL, overlooking the Mid Valley City—which houses two shopping malls, hotels, offices and apartments—just across the River Klang.

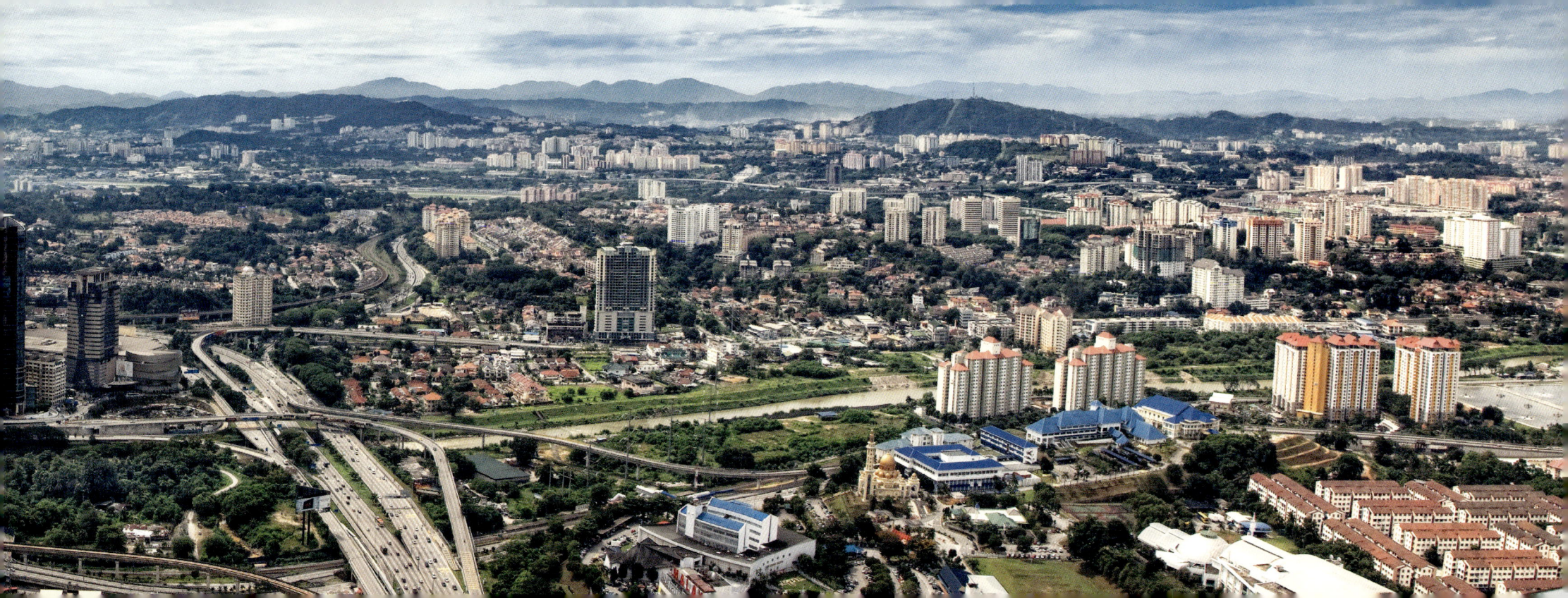

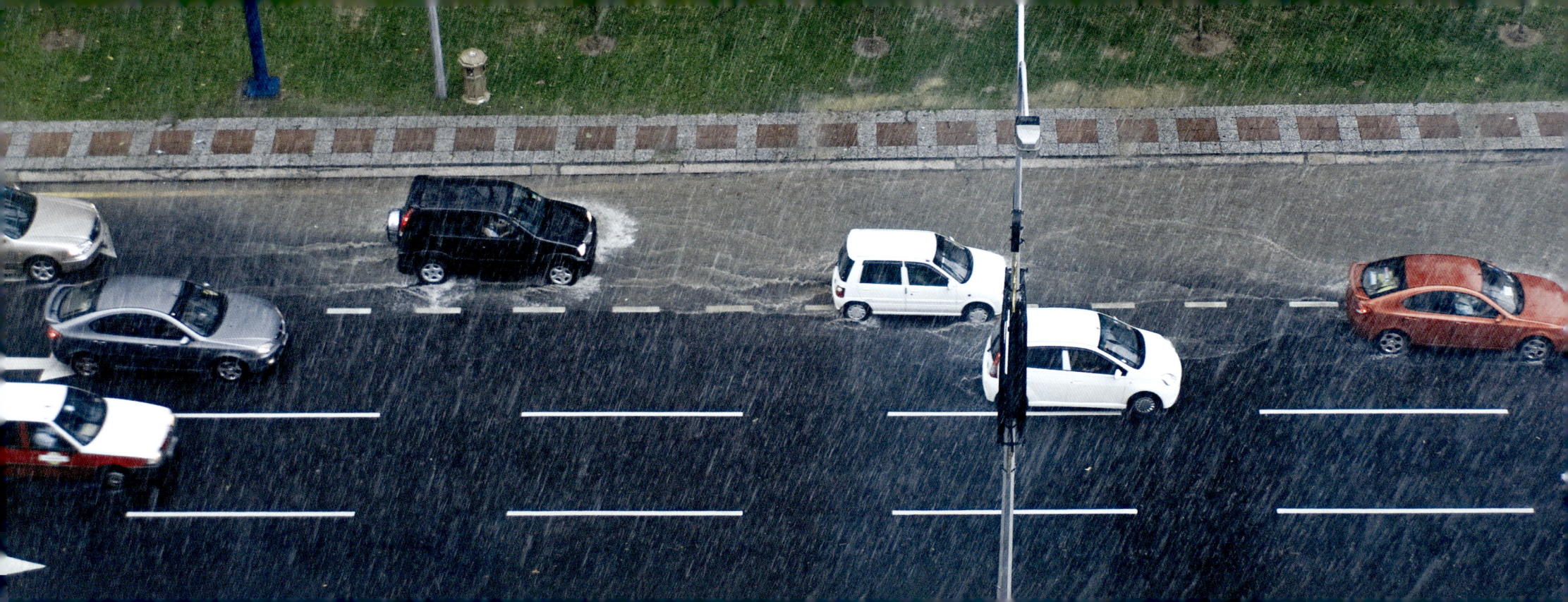

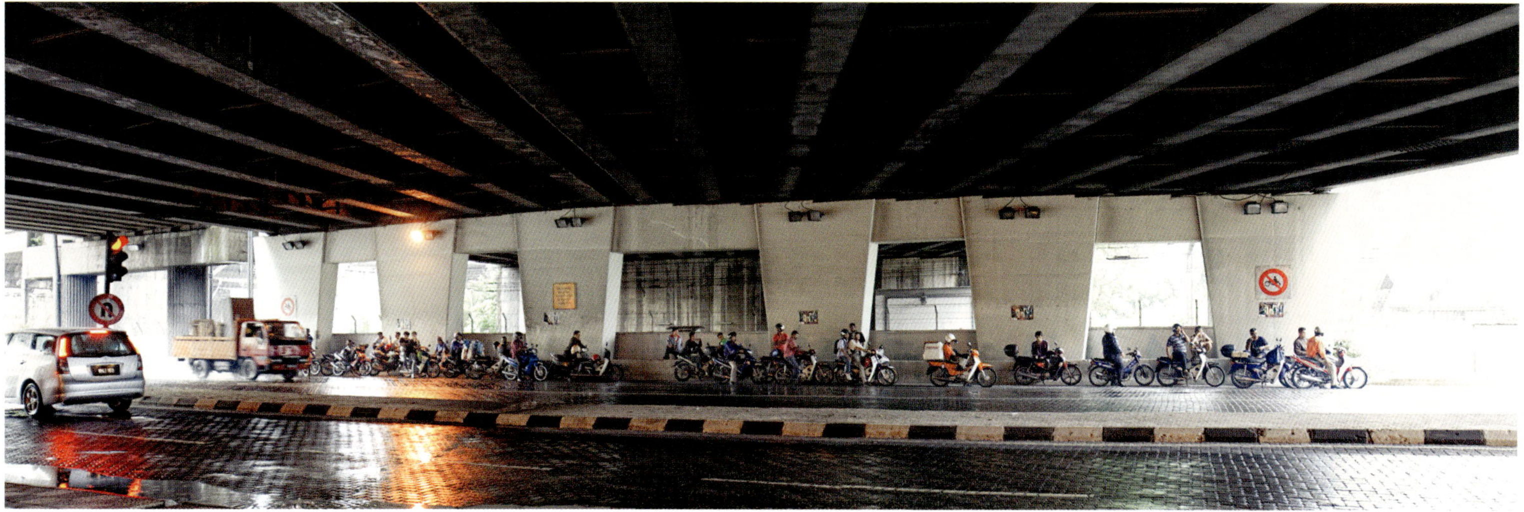

THIS PAGE Motorcyclists sheltera from the rain under a road bridge. OPPOSITE With 230 centimetres of rain annually, KL is one of the wettest cities in the world!

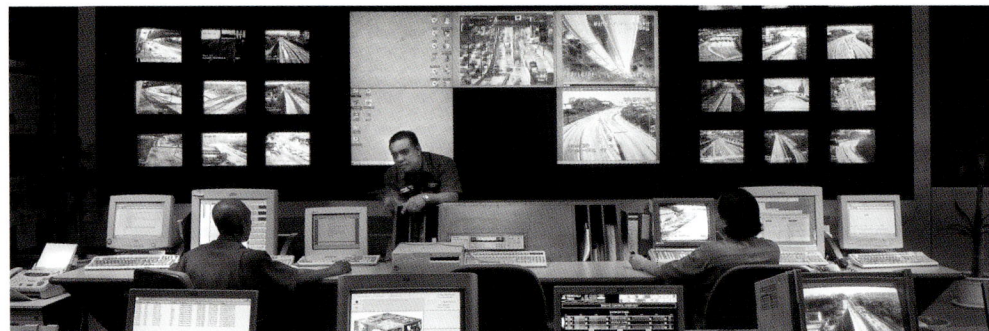

THIS PAGE SPRINT highway traffic monitoring centre. OPPOSITE Evening rush hour traffic at the Lebuhraya Damansara–Puchong (LDP) toll at Sunway, a suburb of Kuala Lumpur.

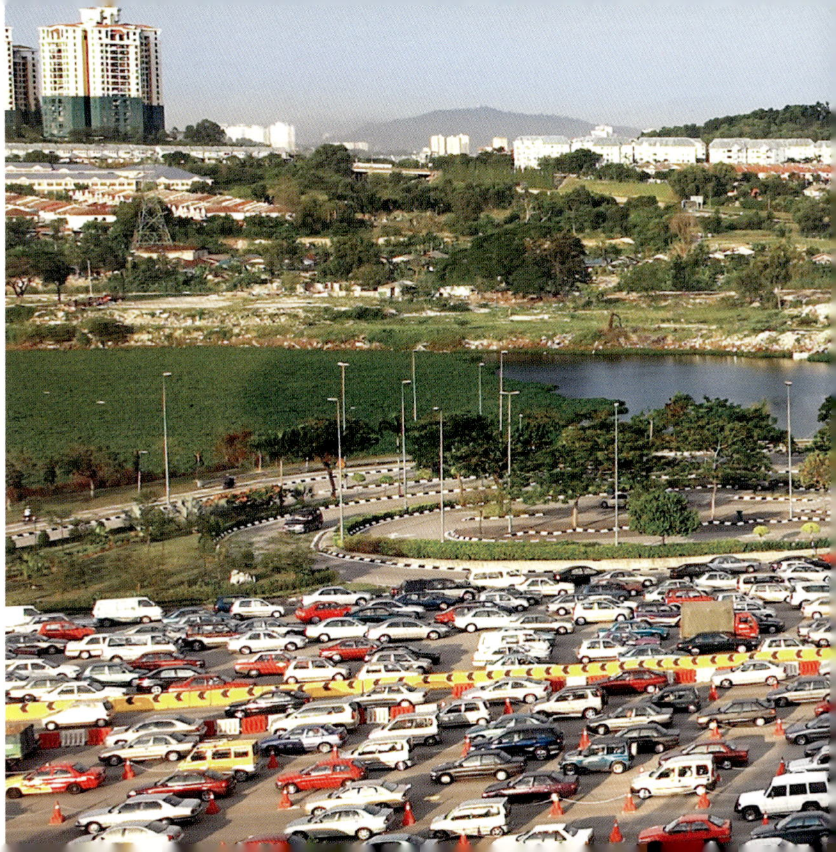

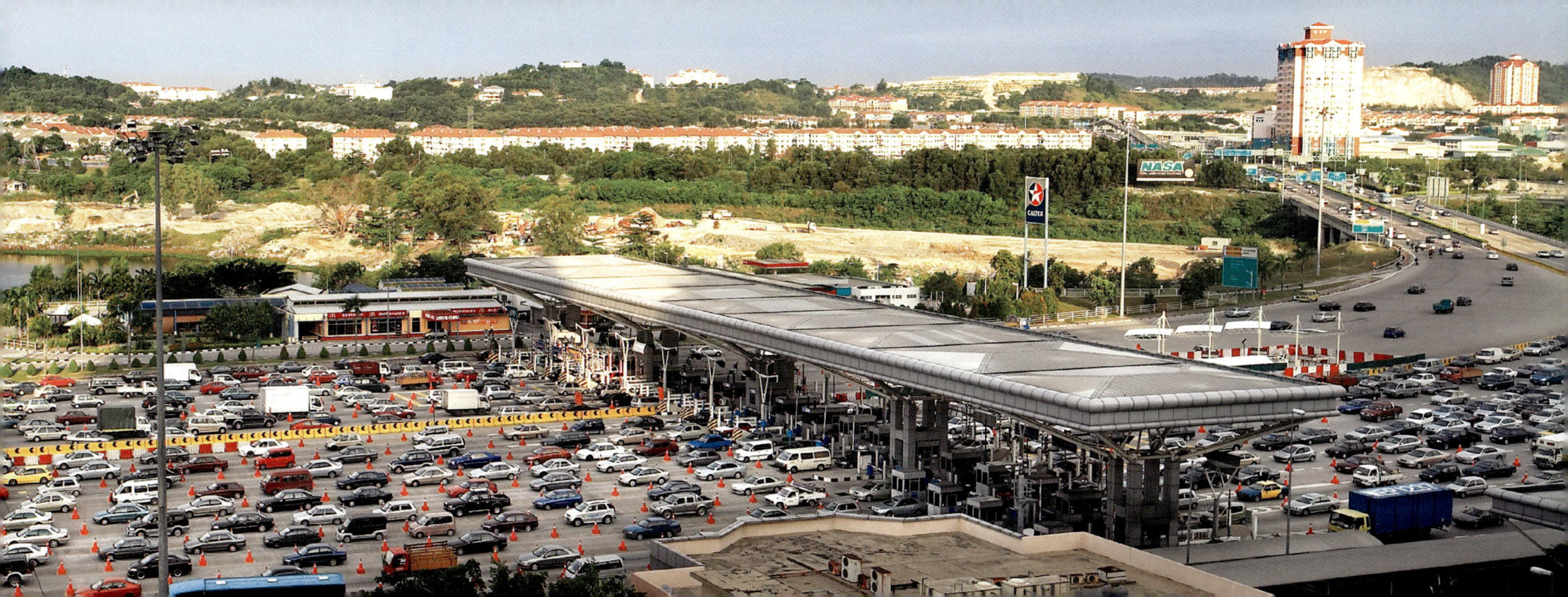

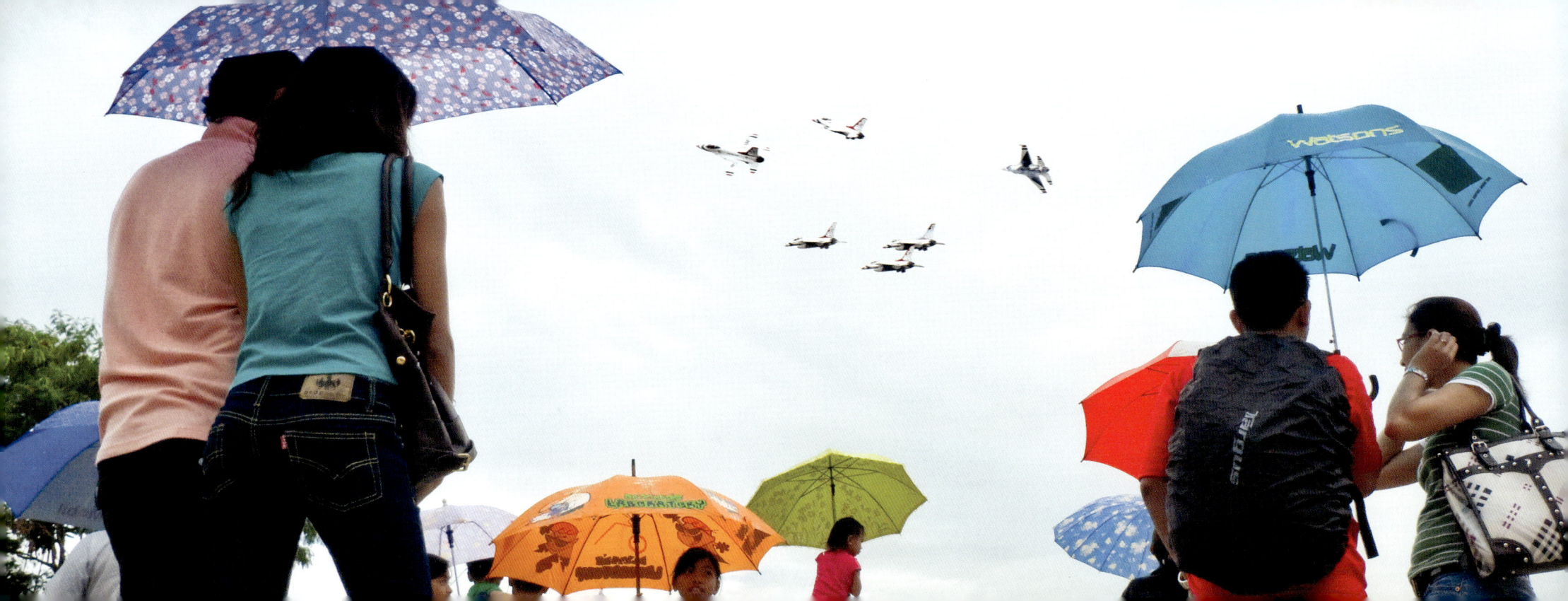

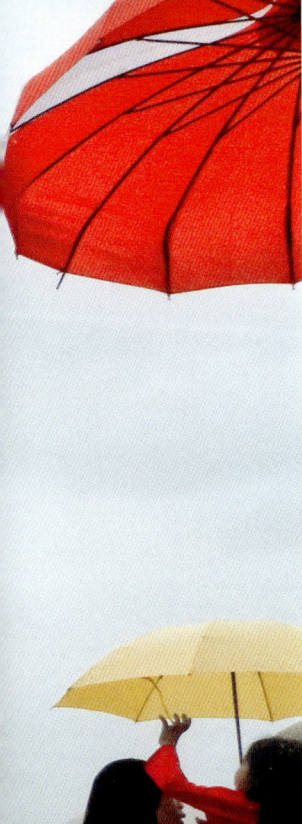

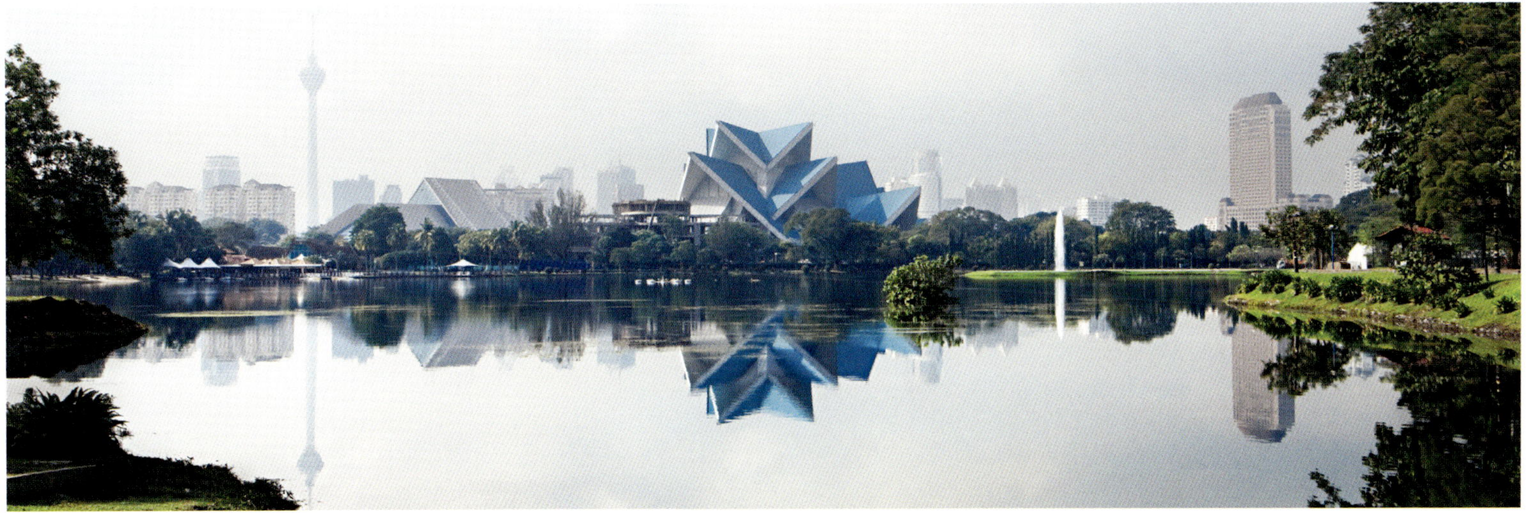

THIS PAGE Seen across Lake Titiwangsa, a rehabilitated mining pool, the Istana Budaya (National Theatre) literally means 'palace of culture'. It stages mainly musicals.
OPPOSITE Malaysians stare in shock and awe at the United States Air Force (USAF) Thunderbirds' acrobatic display at the Royal Malaysian Air Force (RMAF) Subang airbase.

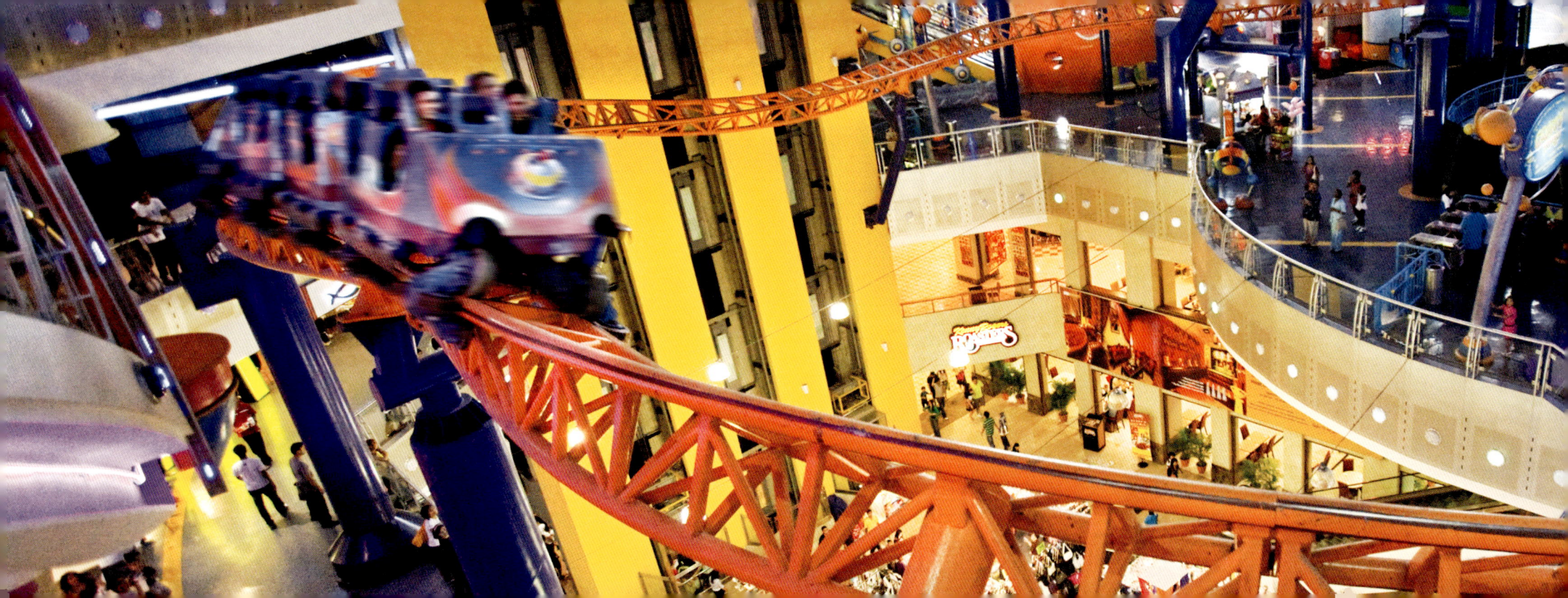

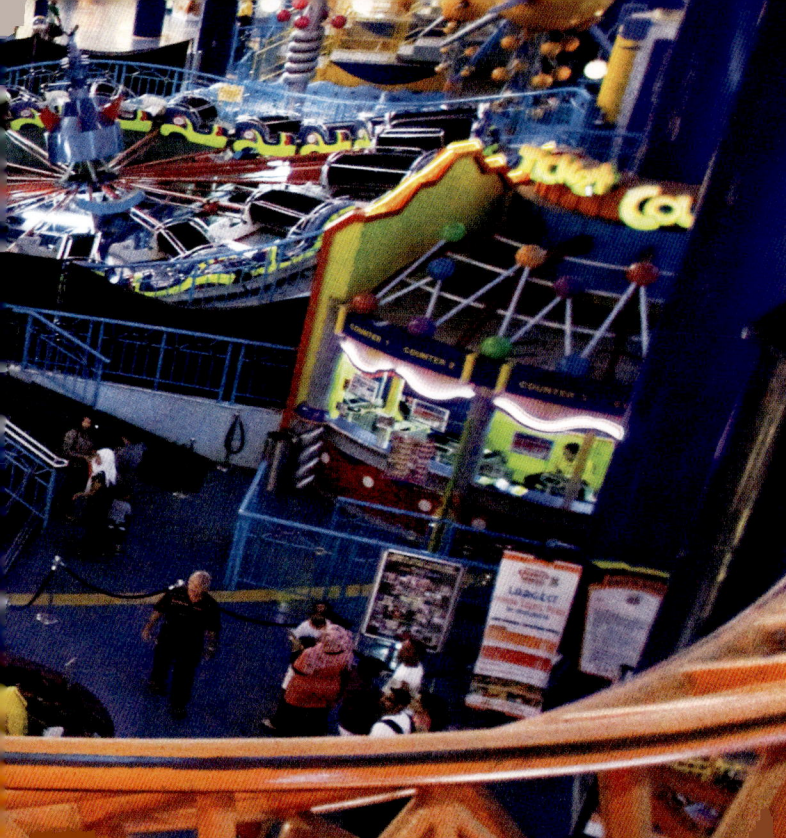

THIS PAGE Roller-coaster ride inside Berjaya Times Square, which is one of KL's bigger shopping malls. It is located in the 'Golden Triangle', the shopping heart of the city, where almost anything can be obtained for a price.

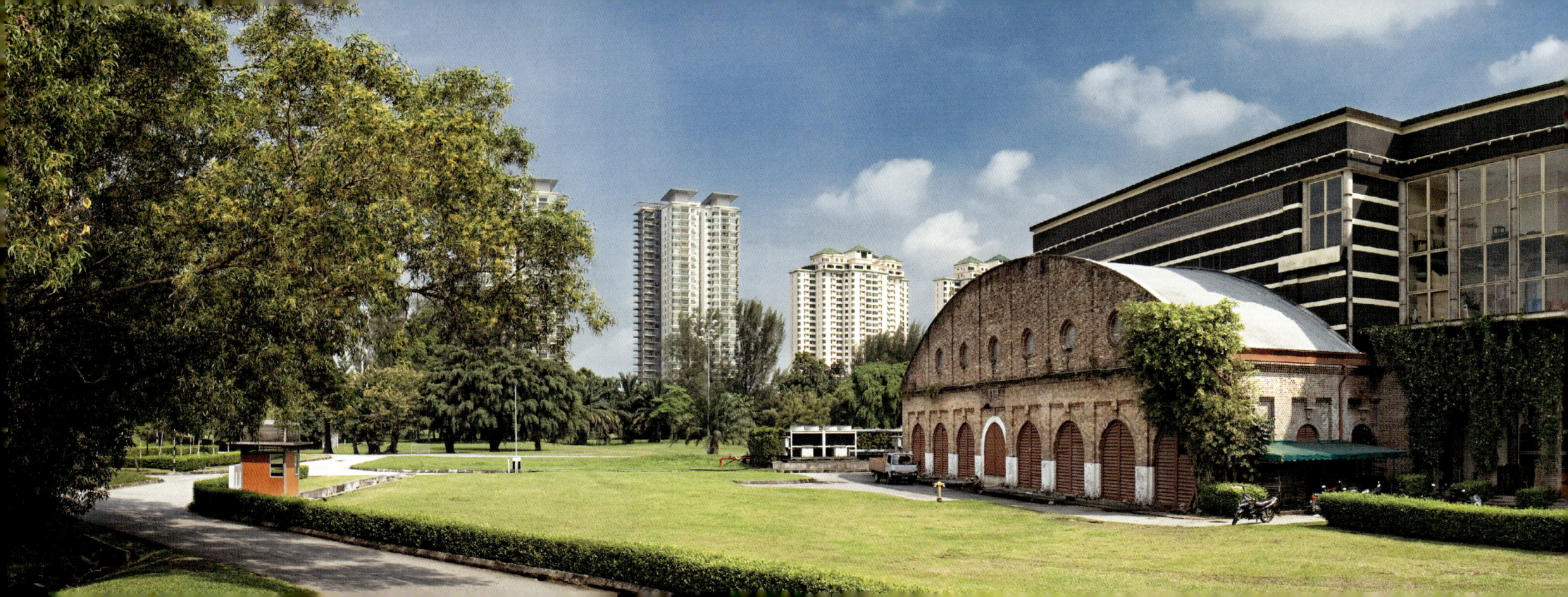

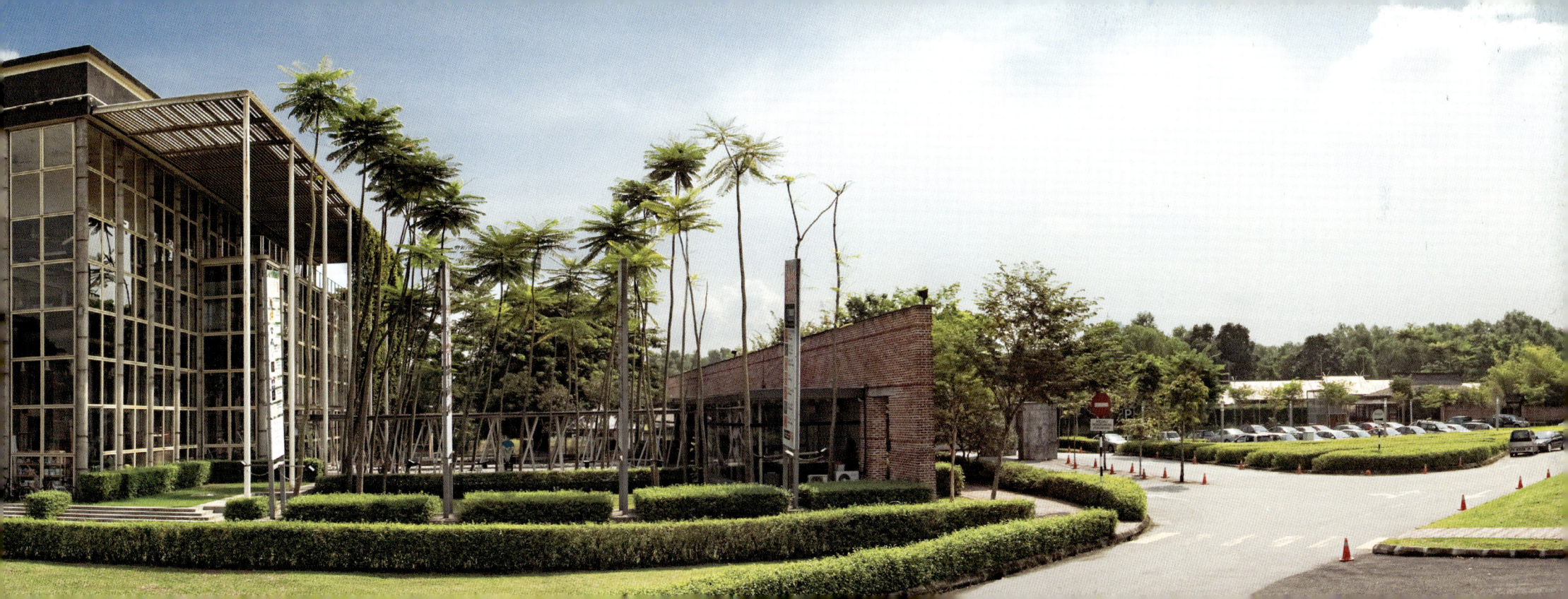

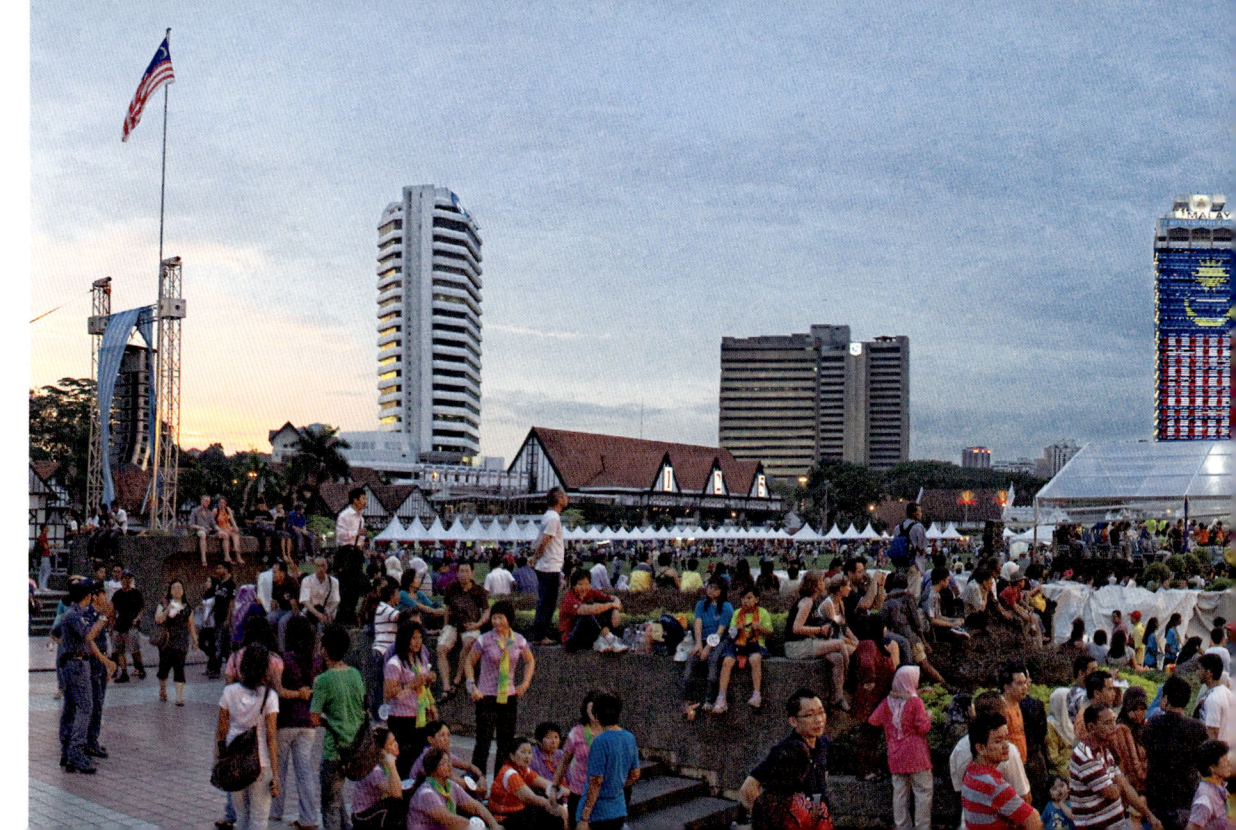

PAGES 70–71 KLPAC, the Kuala Lumpur Performing Arts Centre, in Sentul West, formerly a train maintenance yard. THIS PAGE Performers and spectators in front of the Sultan Abdul Samad Building at Dataran Merdeka during the 2010 Colours of Malaysia cultural event.

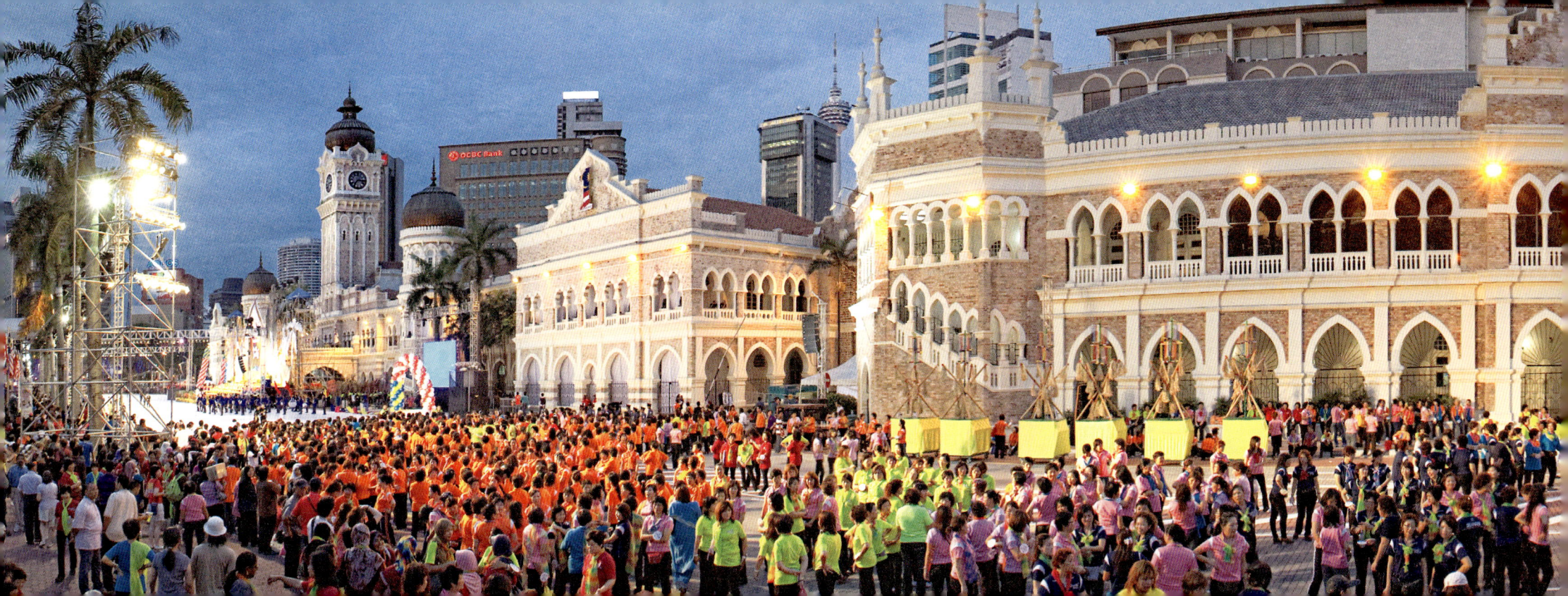

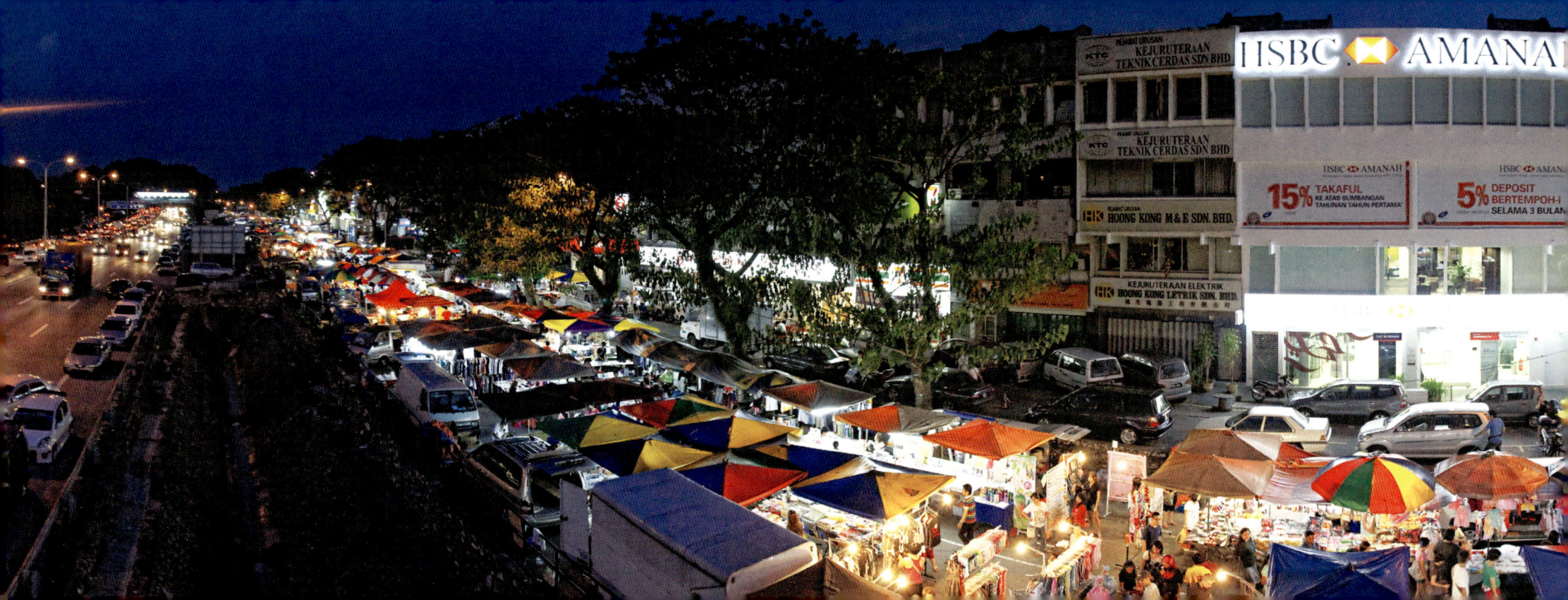

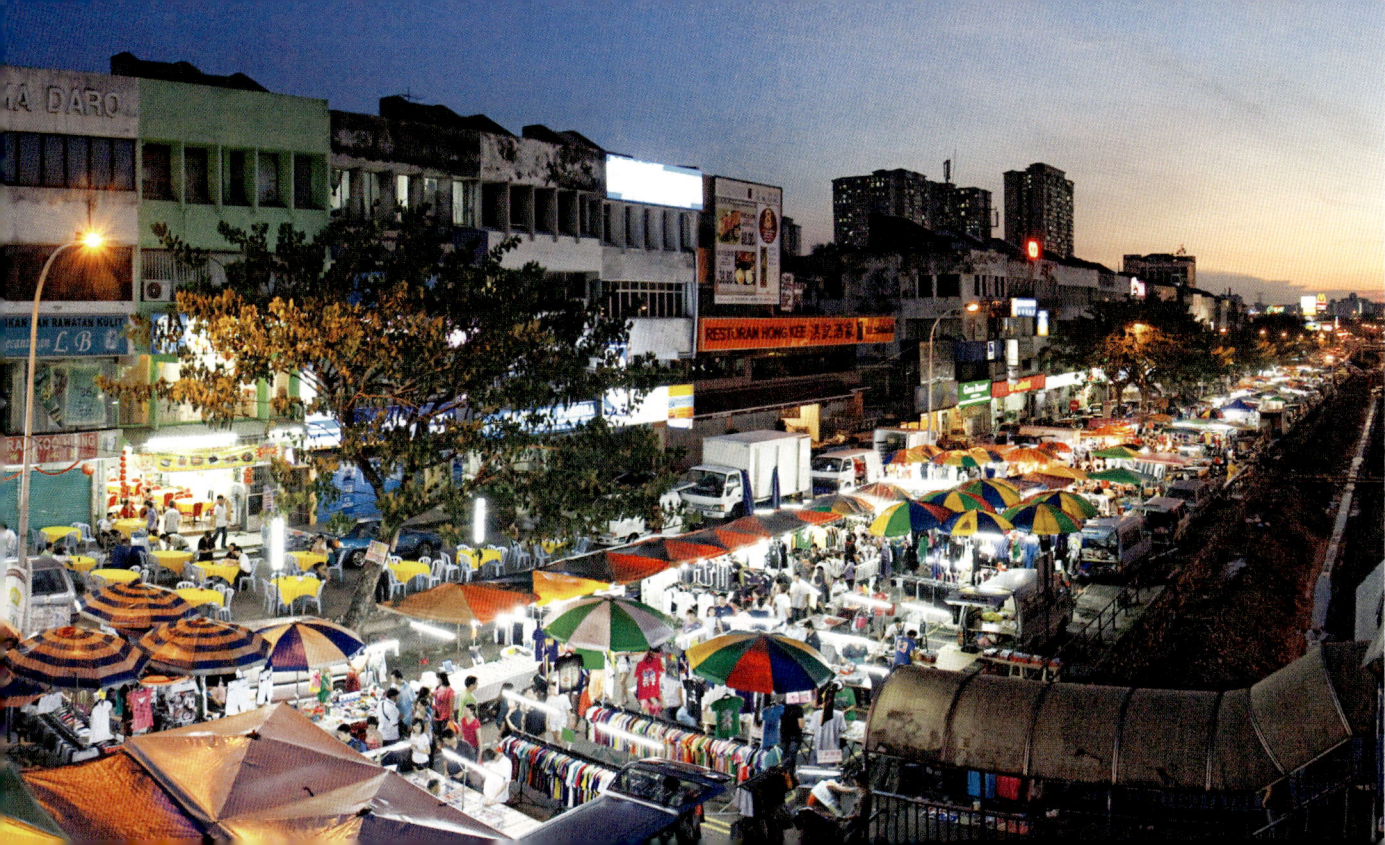

THIS PAGE There are weekly *pasar malam* (night markets) in hundreds of locations around the city and beyond, although most are not as long as this one in Taman Connaught. They sell mainly food, but clothes and toys are common, too.

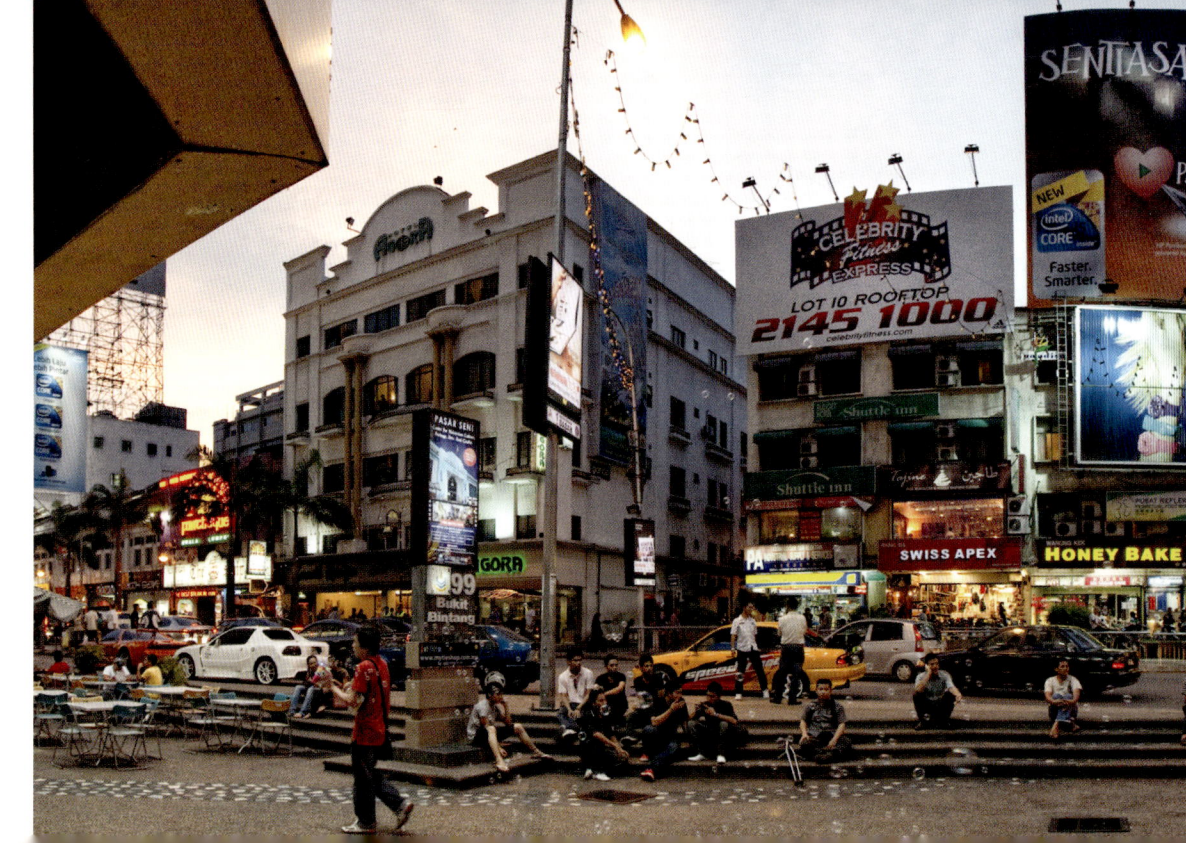

THIS PAGE The Jalan Bukit Bintang–Jalan Sultan Ismail junction outside the Lot 10 shopping mall.

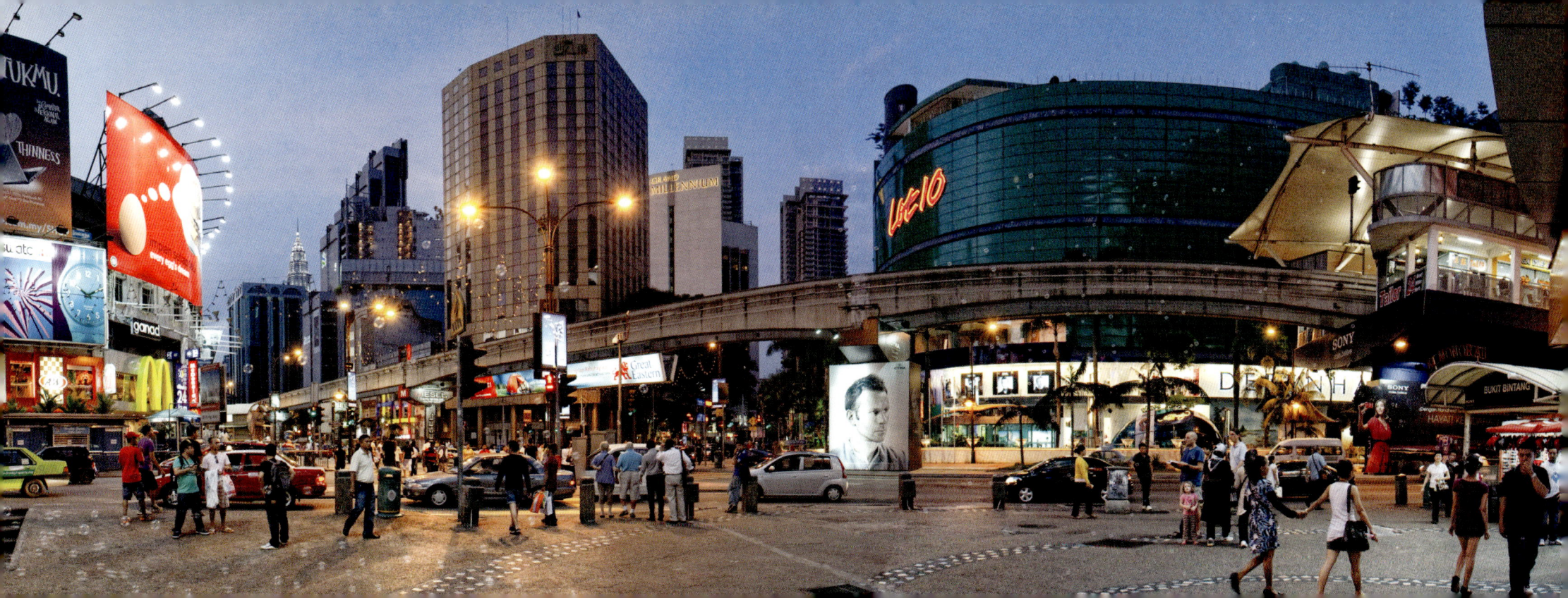

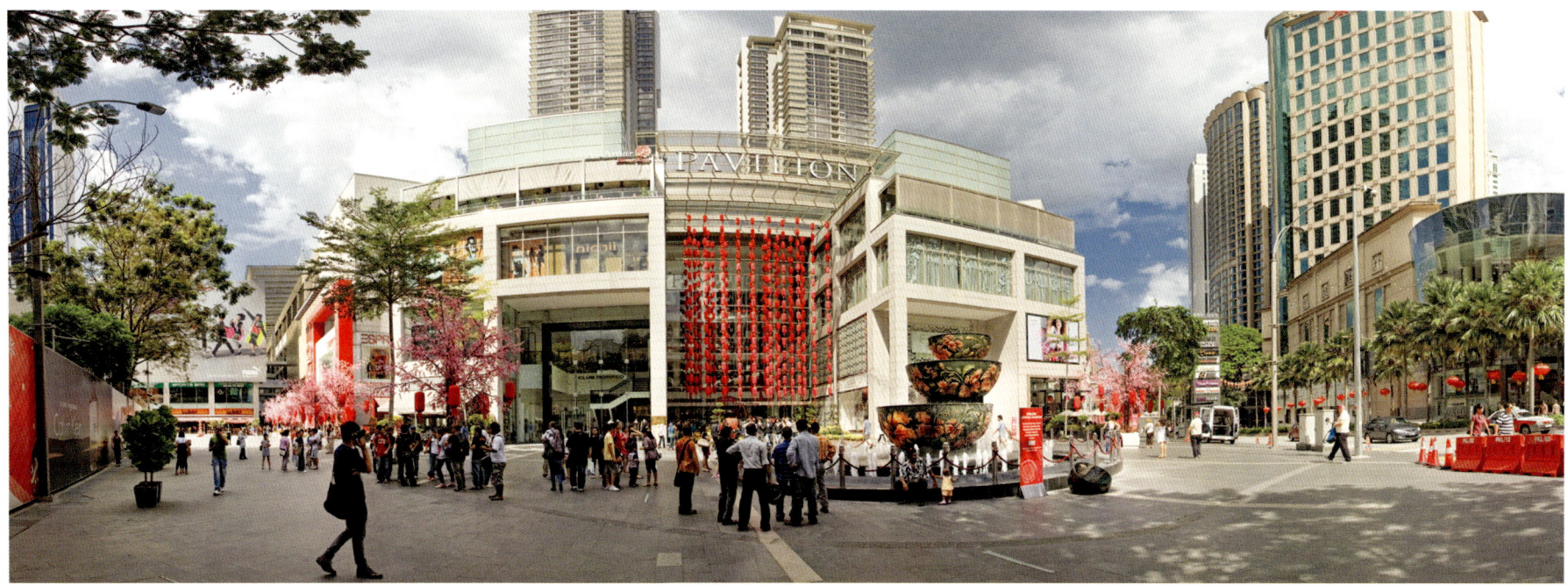

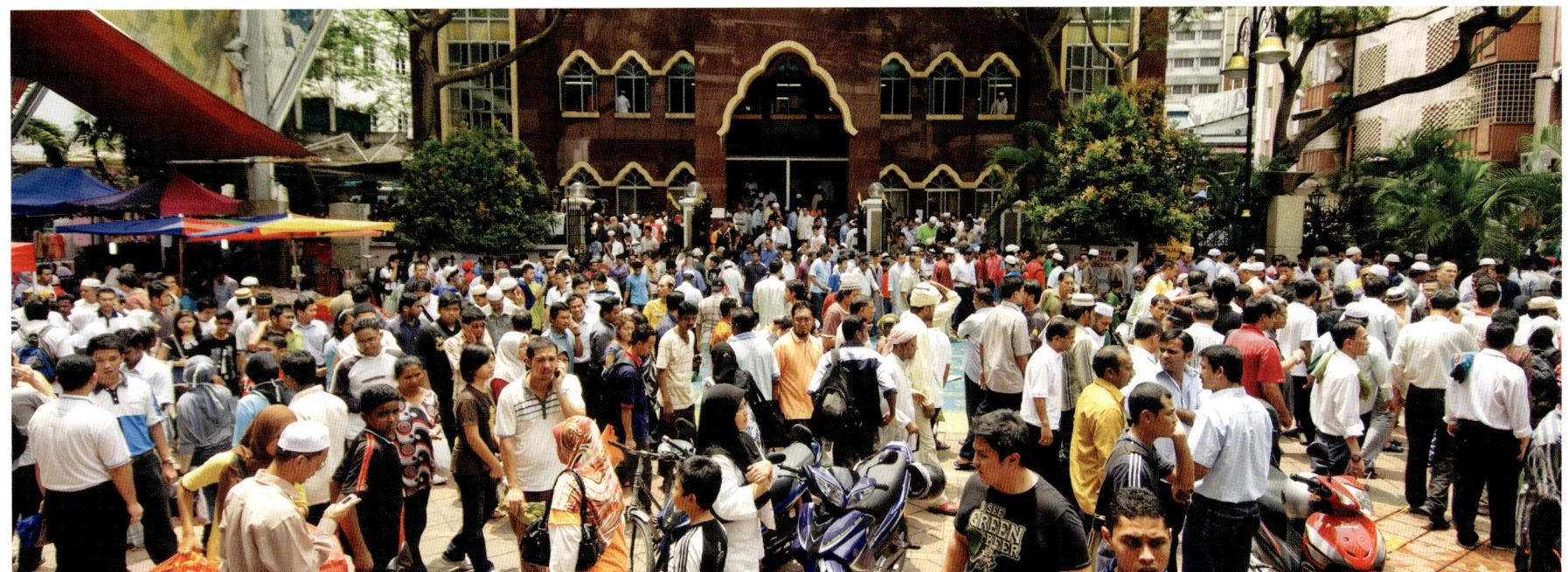

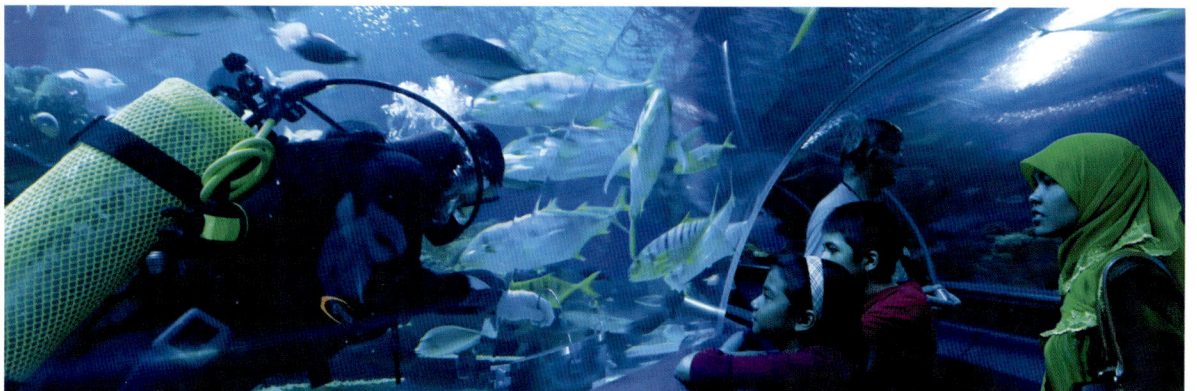

PAGE 78 Shopping in the new Pavilion mall, which was built after the Bukit Bintang Girls' School was demolished. PAGE 79 More shoppers at the older area of Jalan Masjid India, known for its Indian Muslim traders. THIS PAGE The underground Aquaria, part of the greater KLCC complex. OPPOSITE Luna Bar, which commands a premium view of the KLCC, to remind people of the offices that they have just escaped from.

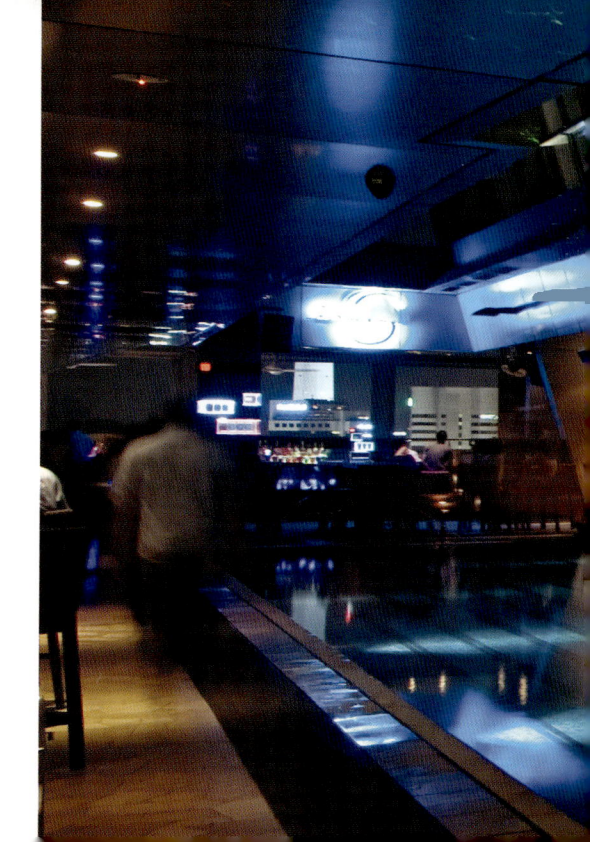

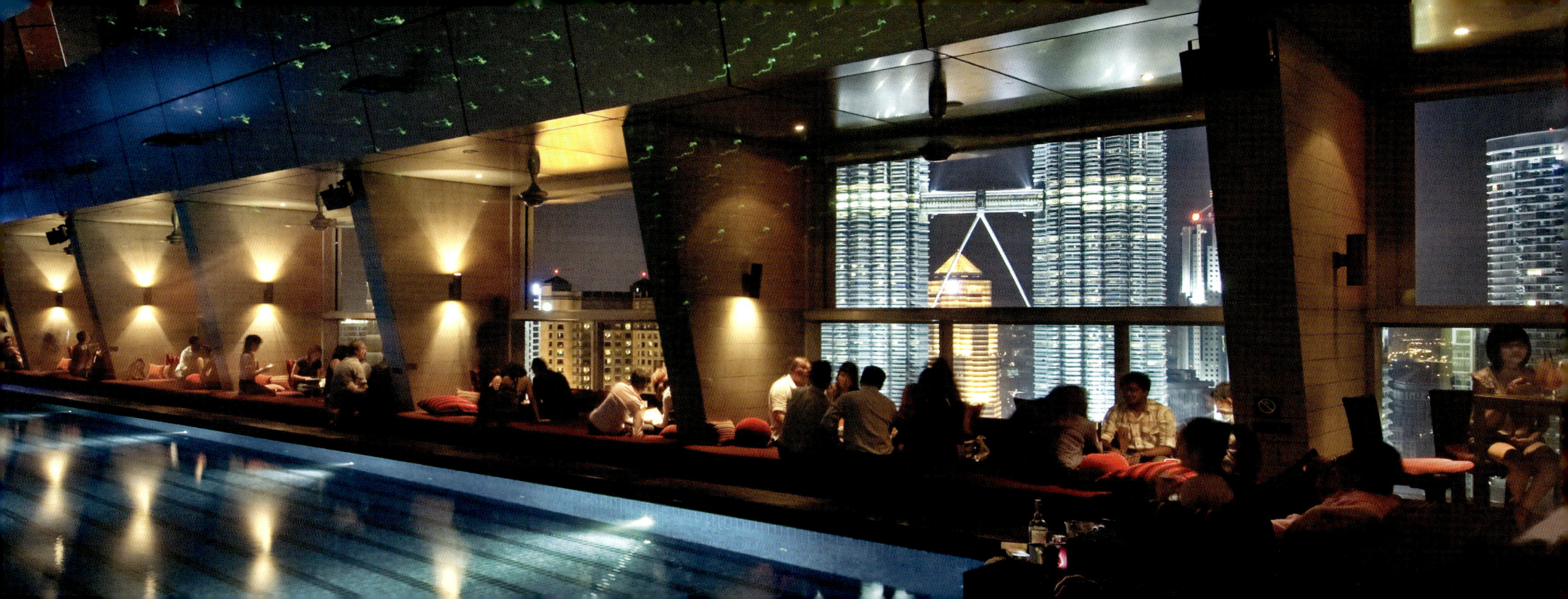

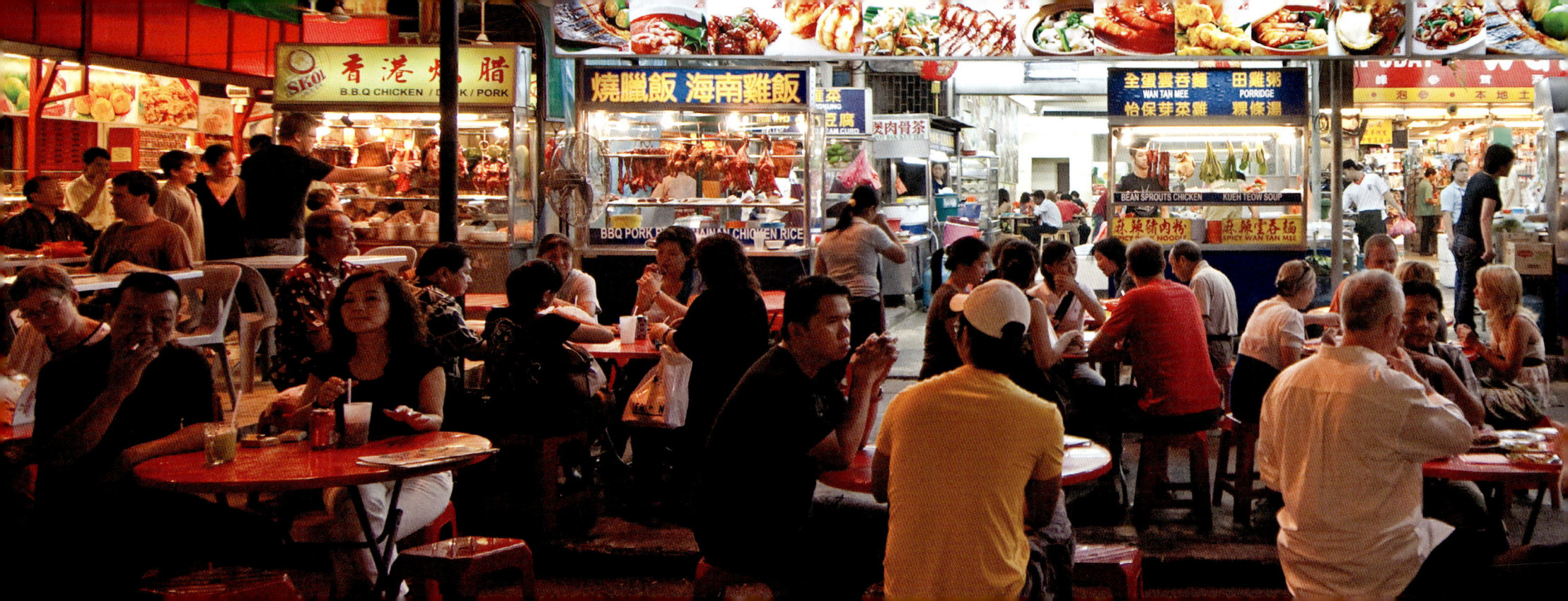

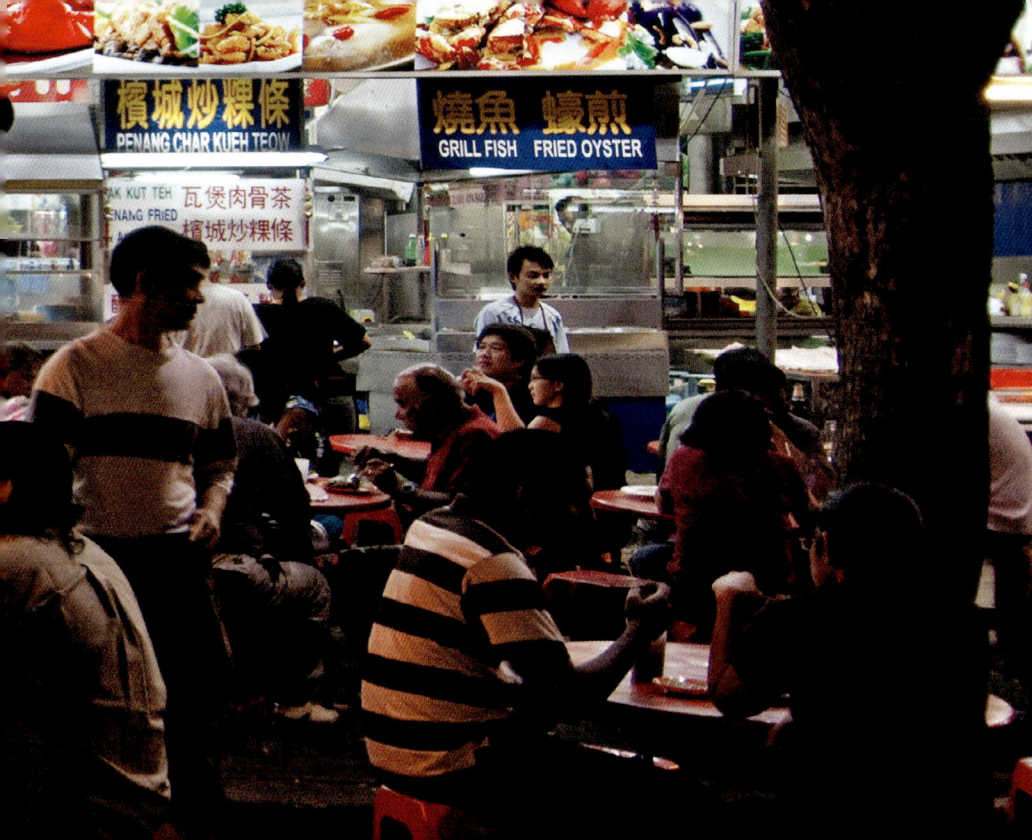

THIS PAGE Outdoor eateries in Jalan Alor. The food here is predominately Chinese. But befitting the 'melting pot' nature of the city, many other such eateries mix Chinese, Indian, Malay and Western cuisine, the proportions depending on which neighbourhood they are located in. Another distinction between the various food courts, aside of course from the quality of what's served, is whether they have fixed or portable objects to sit on.

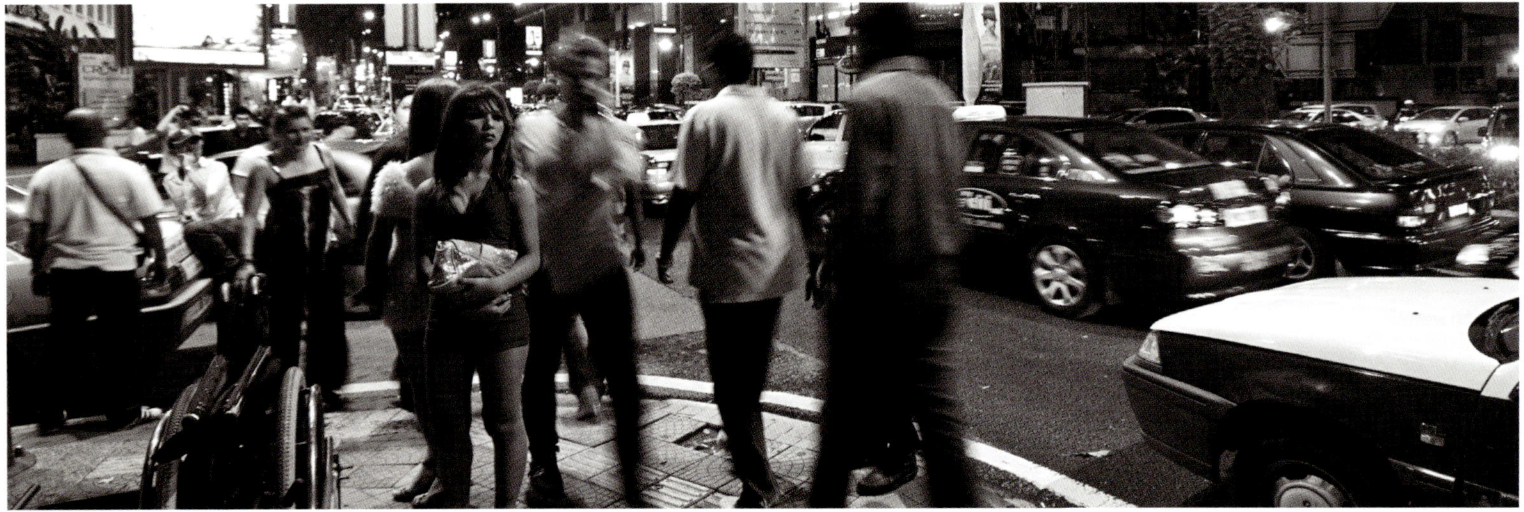

THIS PAGE Pedestrians along Jalan P. Ramlee on a busy weekend night. OPPOSITE Street entertainment in Jalan Bukit Bintang. Some parts of KL also have medicine-selling men with the gift of the gab.

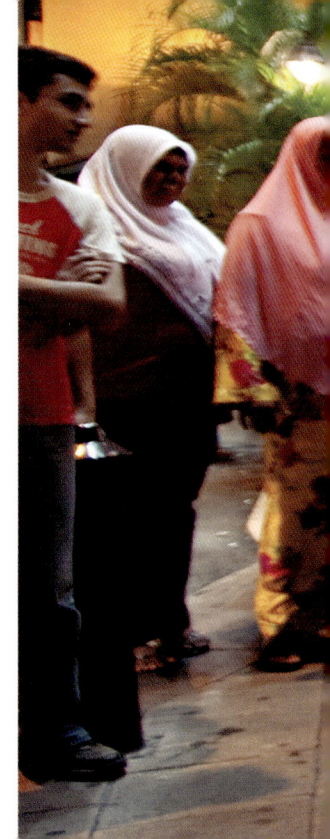

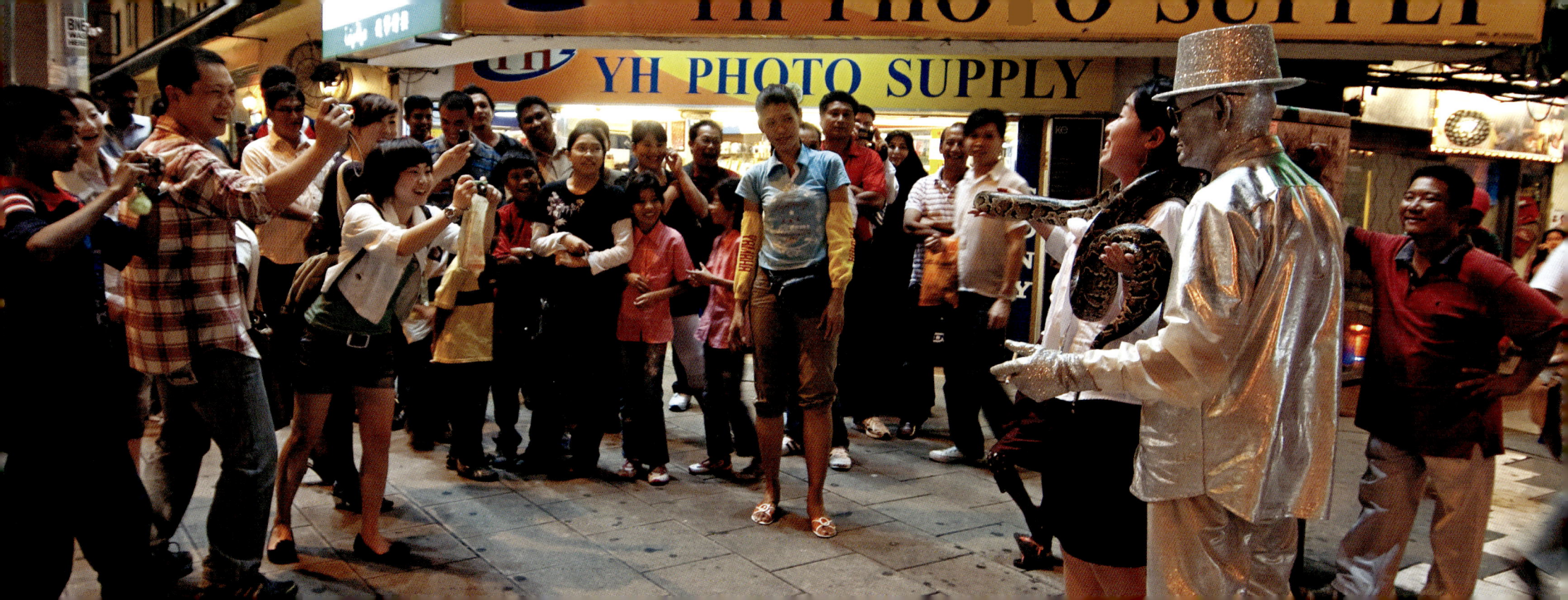

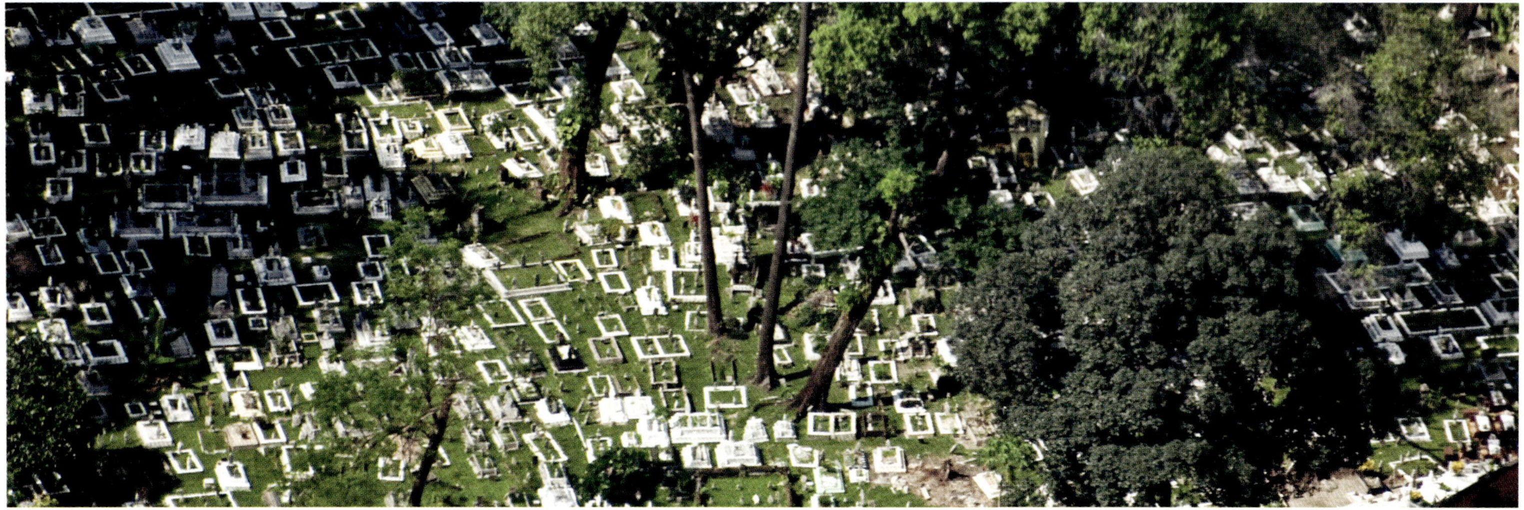

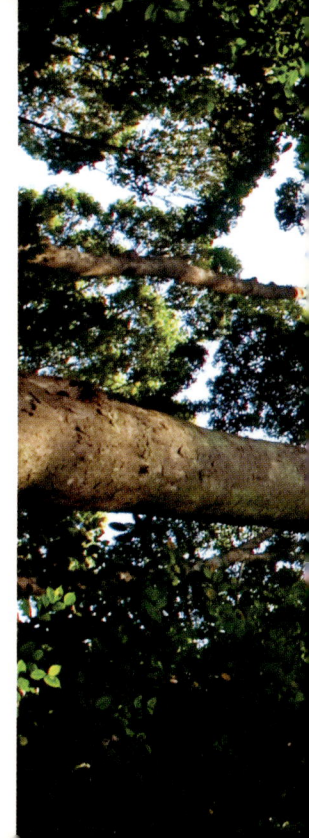

THIS PAGE The Muslim cemetery of Jalan Ampang. Among those buried here is P. Ramlee, Malaysia's most famous entertainer, and the road named after him is not far away. OPPOSITE Looking up at the Forest Research Institute of Malaysia (FRIM), which was founded in 1929 and contains over 15,000 species of plants.

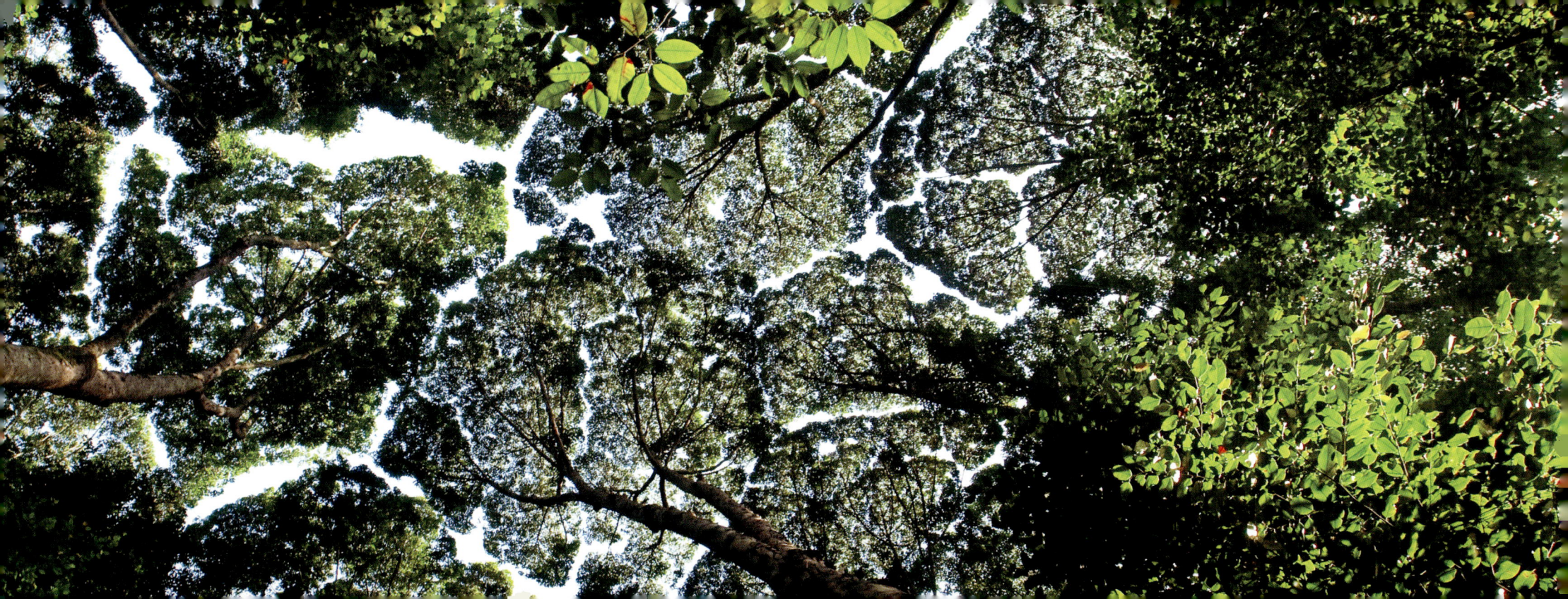

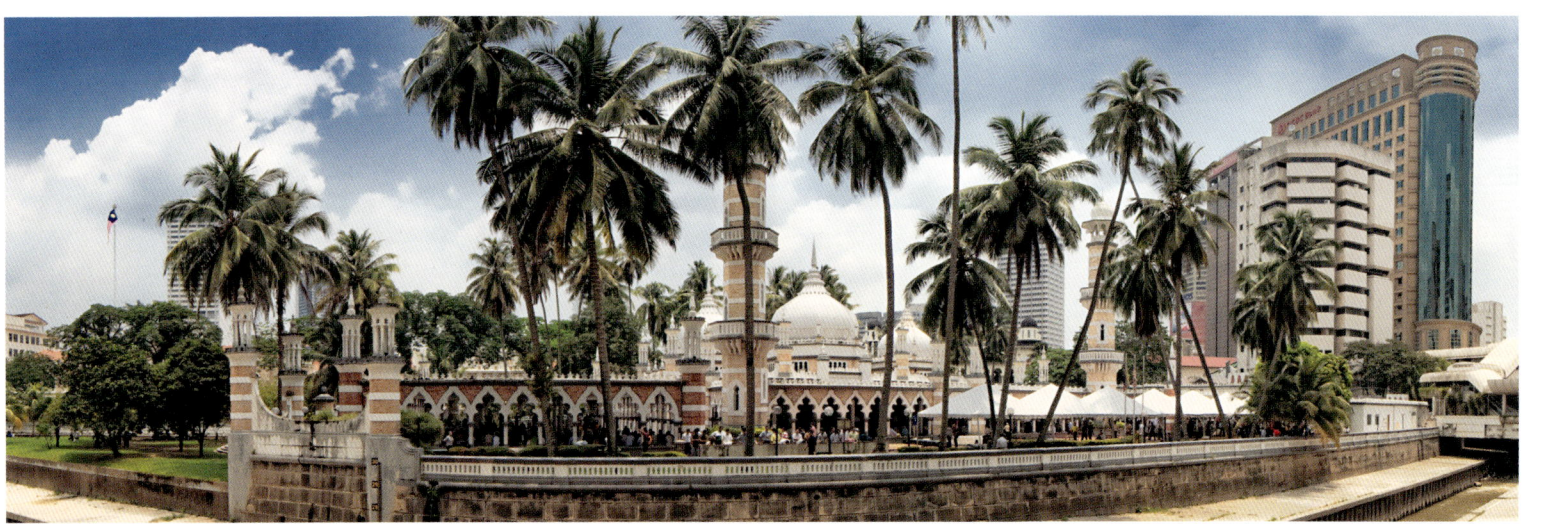

THIS PAGE Masjid Jamek mosque, one of the city's oldest, was built on a Malay burial ground. OPPOSITE Putrajaya Mosque. This shot was not taken on Friday afternoon.

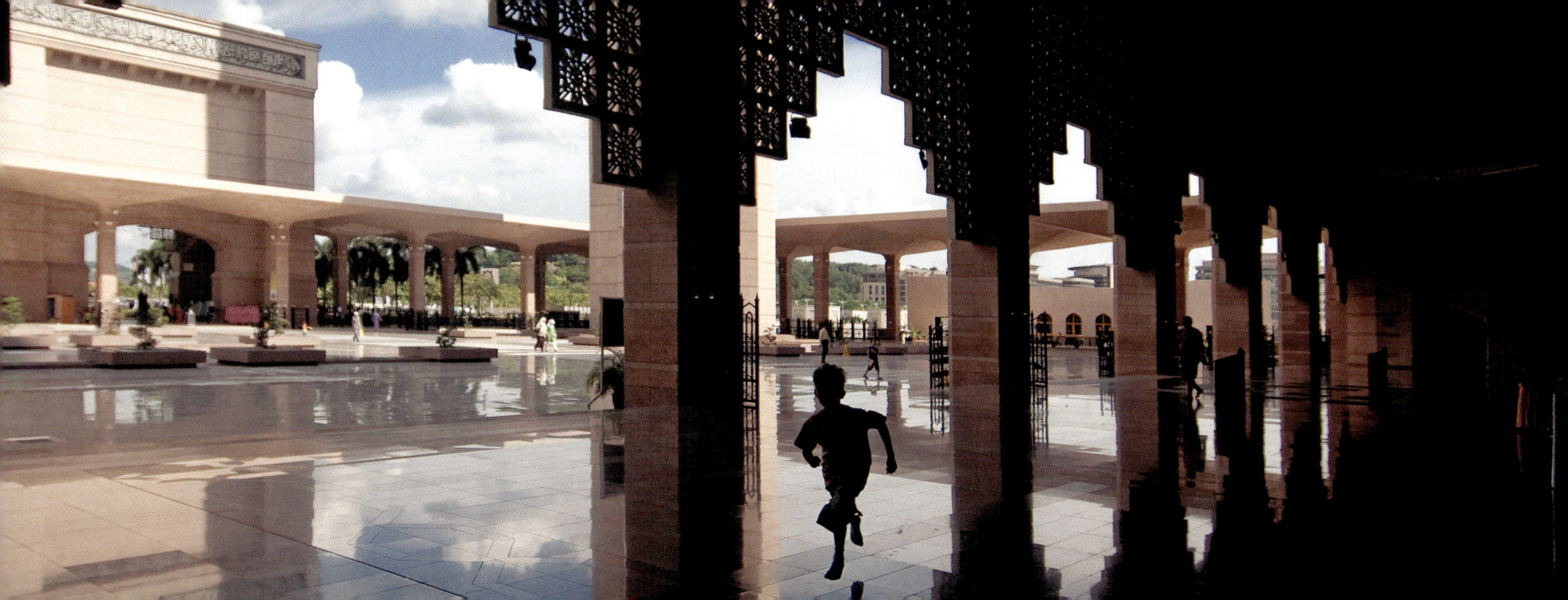

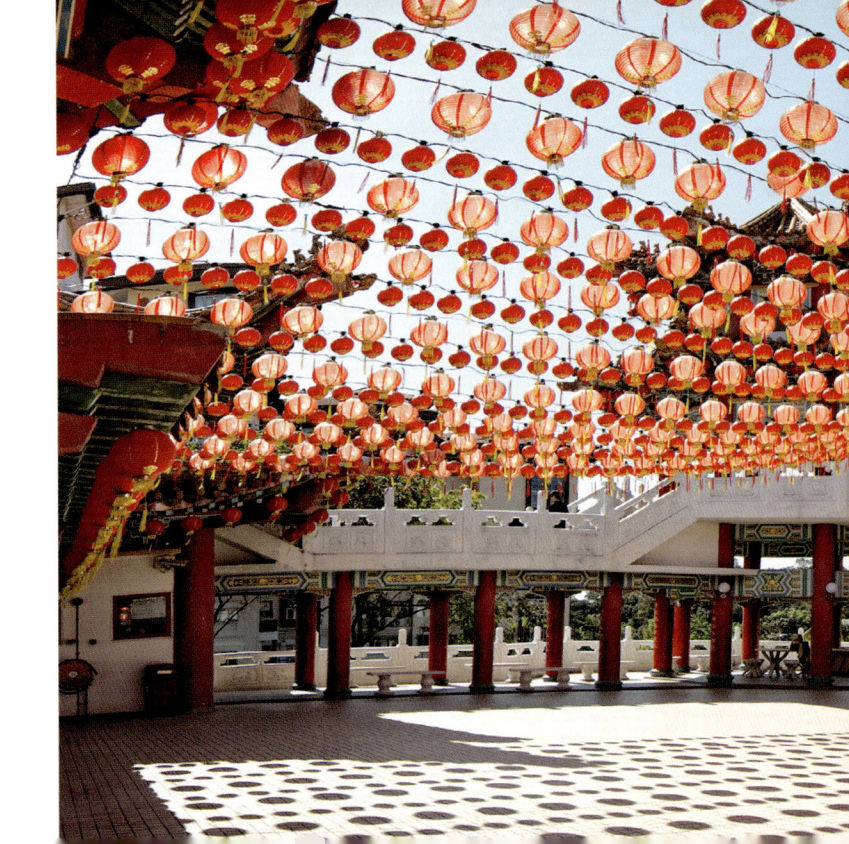

THIS PAGE Thean Hou temple, Taman Seputeh, adorned with lanterns for Chinese New Year.

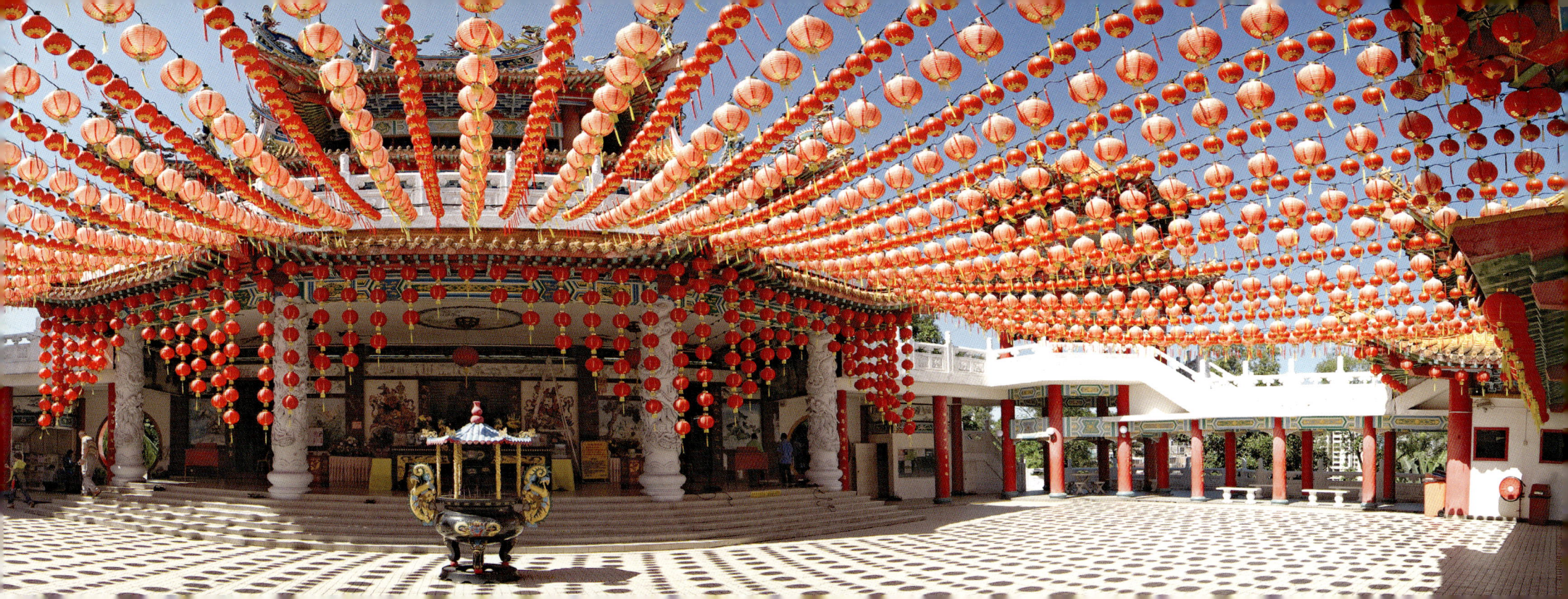

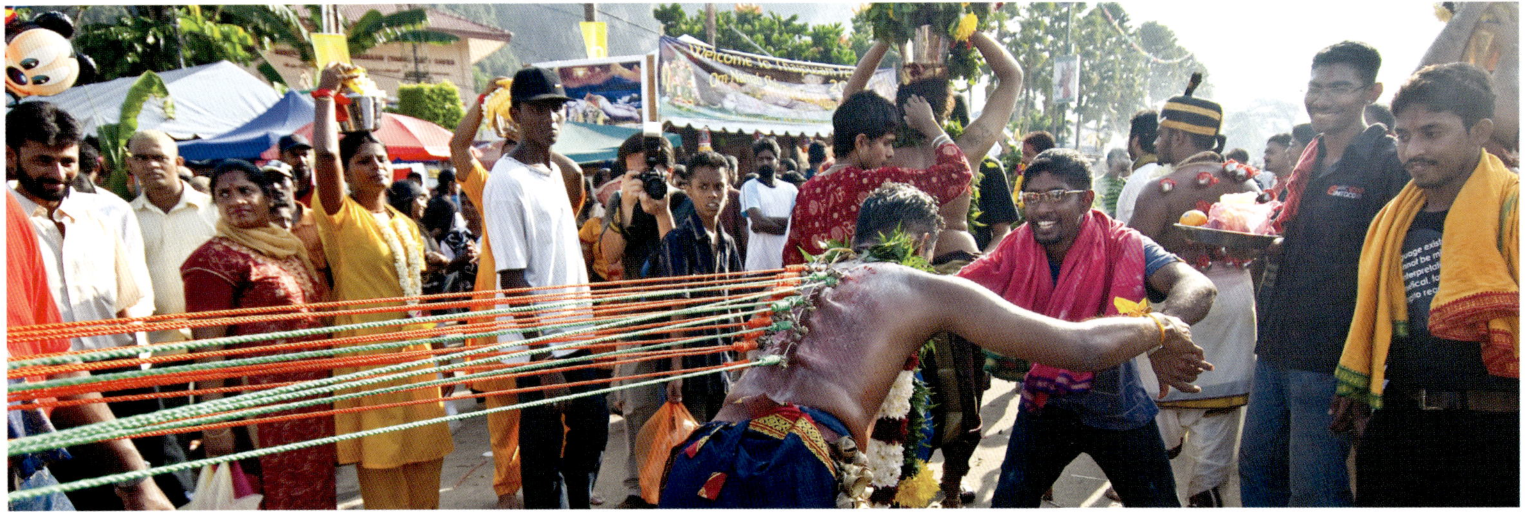

THIS PAGE One of the most colourful events in the Malaysian calendar is the Hindu celebration of Thaipusam in Batu Caves. Pilgrims travel from various countries and number more than a million. The kavadi-bearing devotees, despite the hooks piercing them, feel no pain. Holy ash is sprinkled on the skewers before being removed from their flesh. OPPOSITE Just outside KL, the 42-metre statue of Lord Murugan (completed in 2006) is surrounded by the limestone formations of Batu Caves.

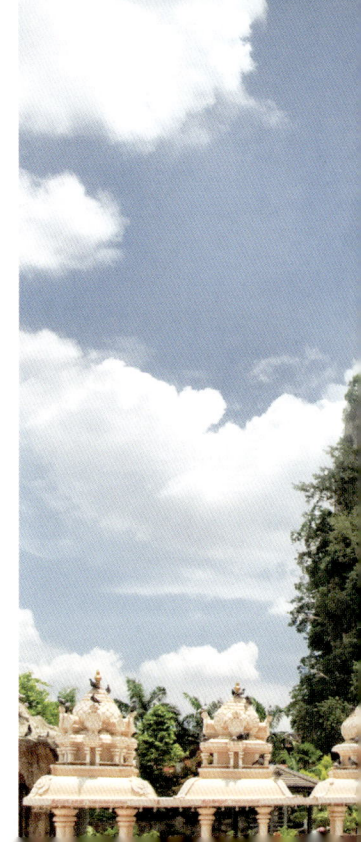

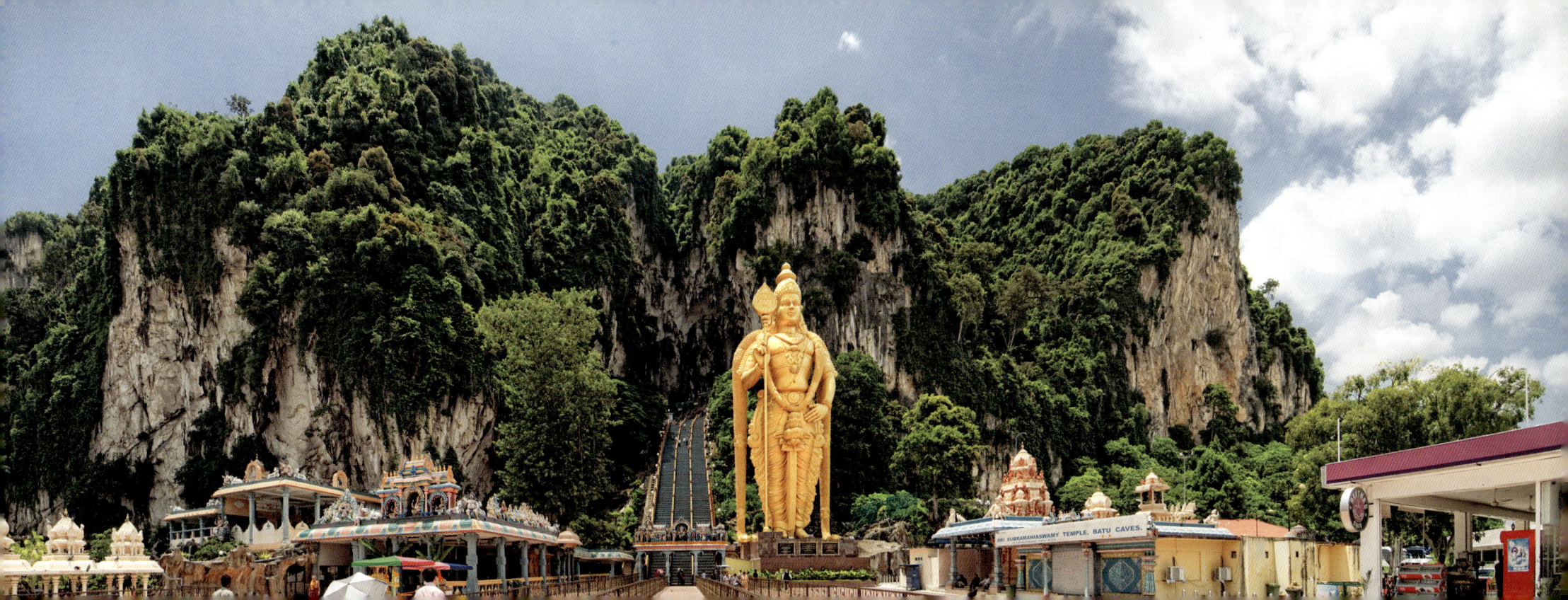

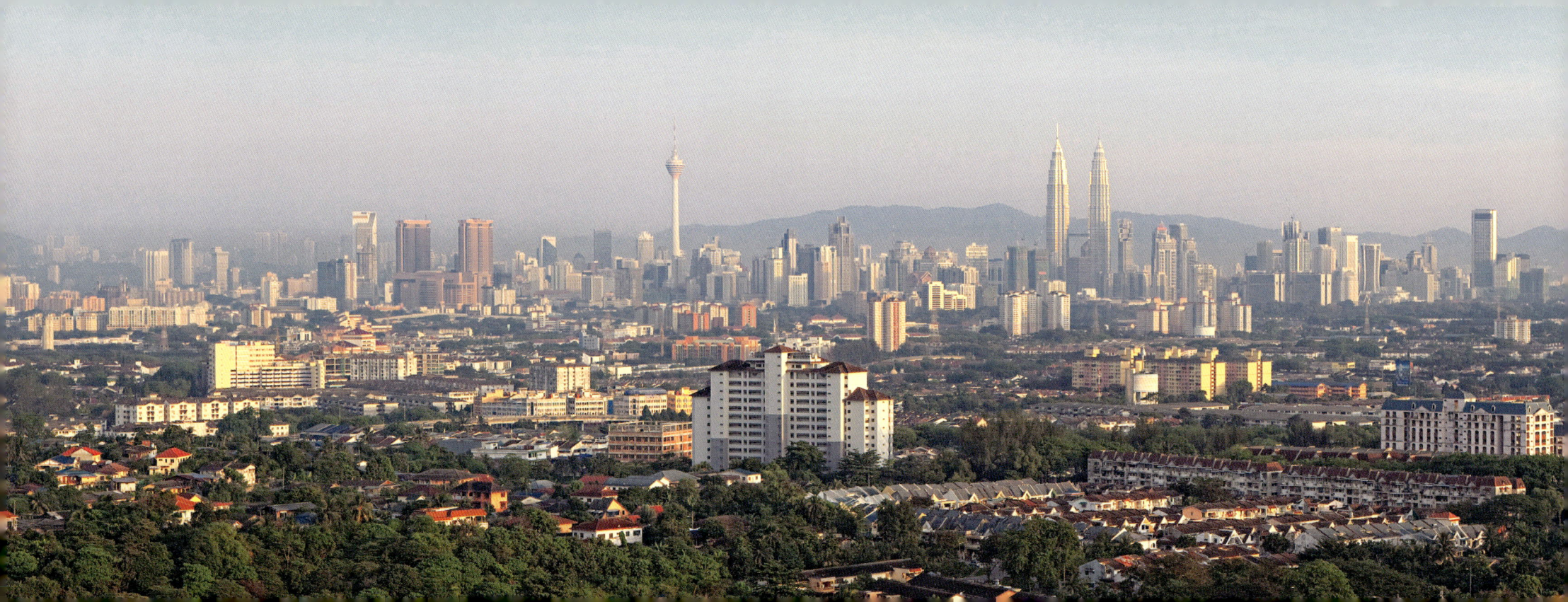

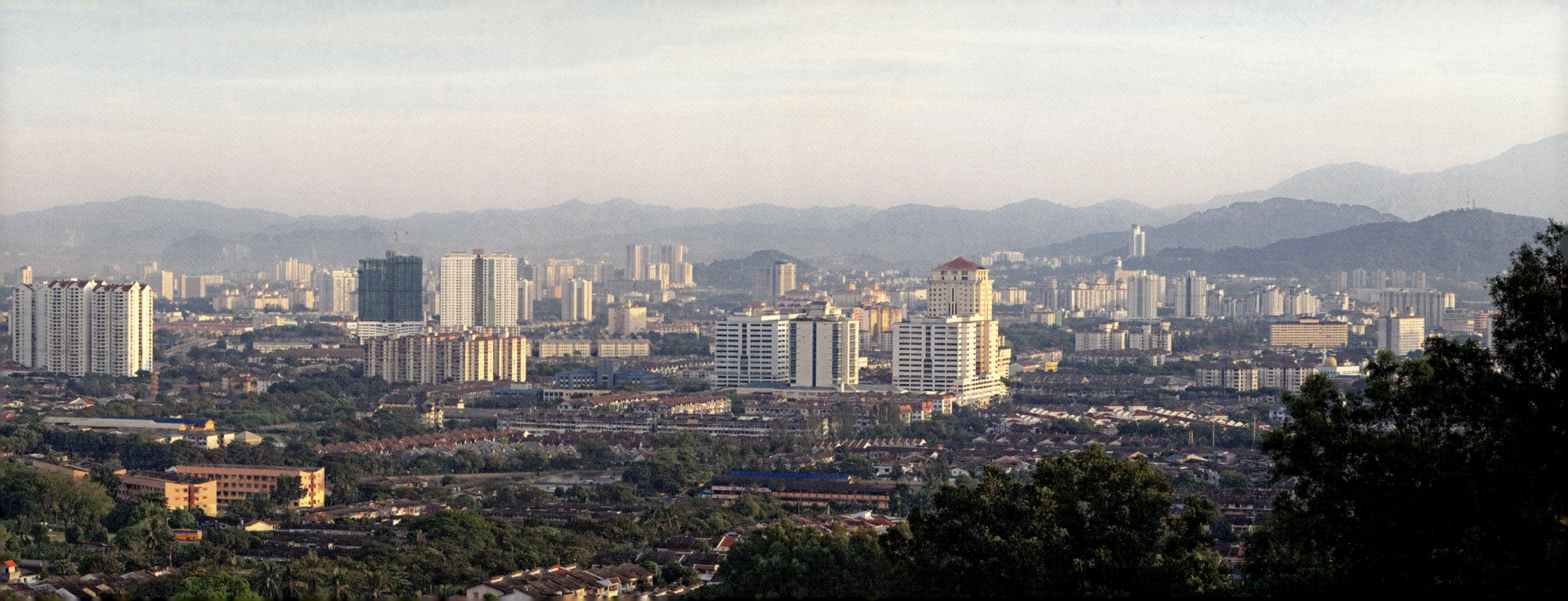

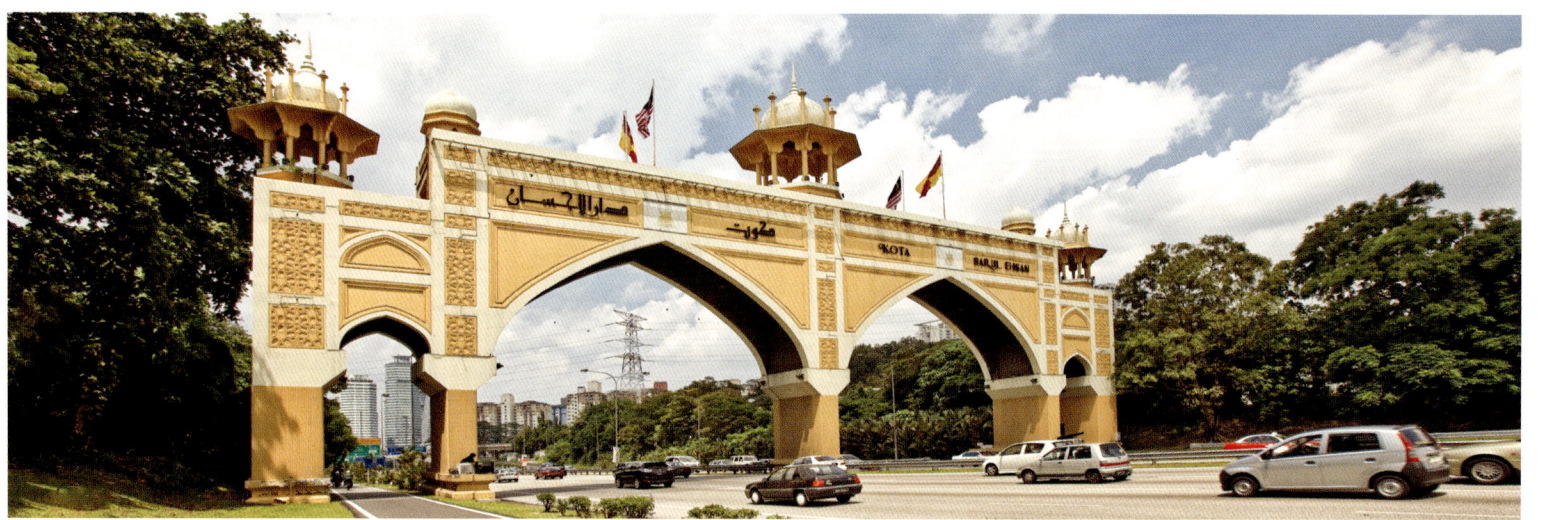

PAGES 94–95 The KL skyline as seen from a hill in Cheras. THIS PAGE Joined at the hip with KL is the satellite city of Petaling Jaya, or PJ. The Kota Darul Ehsan arch on the Federal Highway is the gateway to that city and also the state of Selangor. OPPOSITE A rainy evening along the Damansara–Puchong highway which also connects KL and PJ.

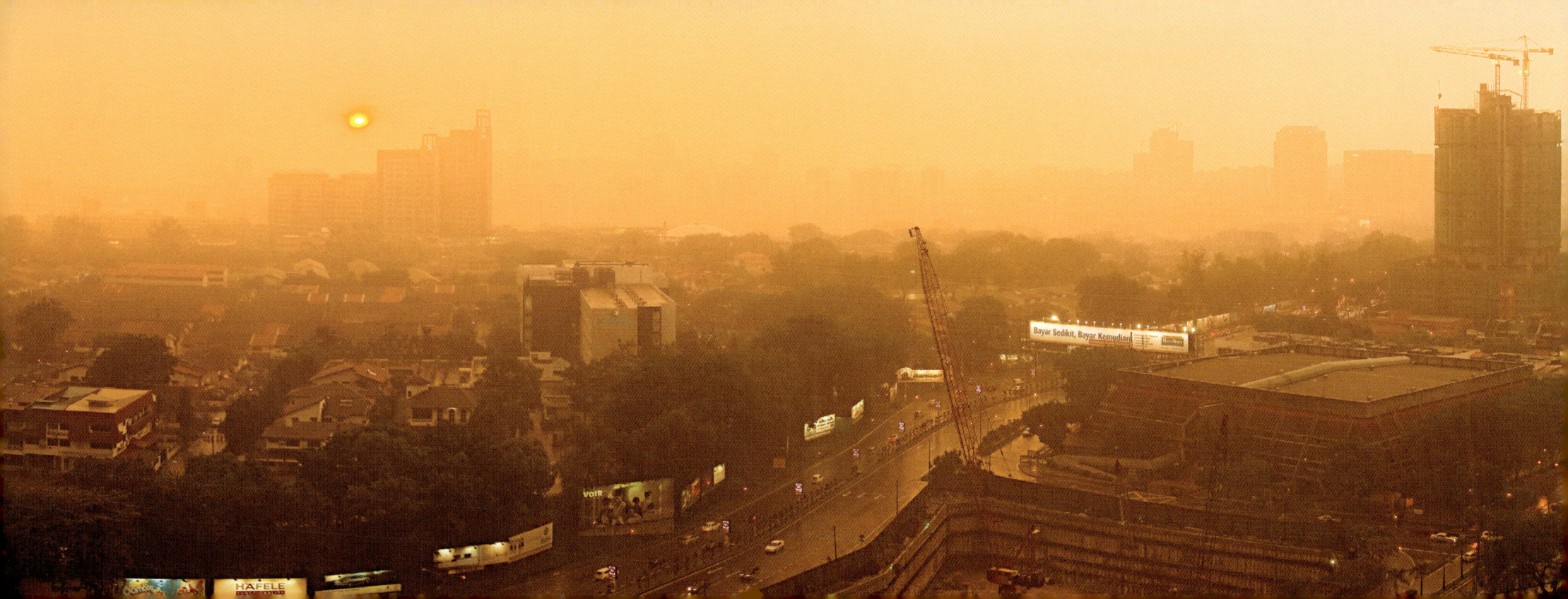

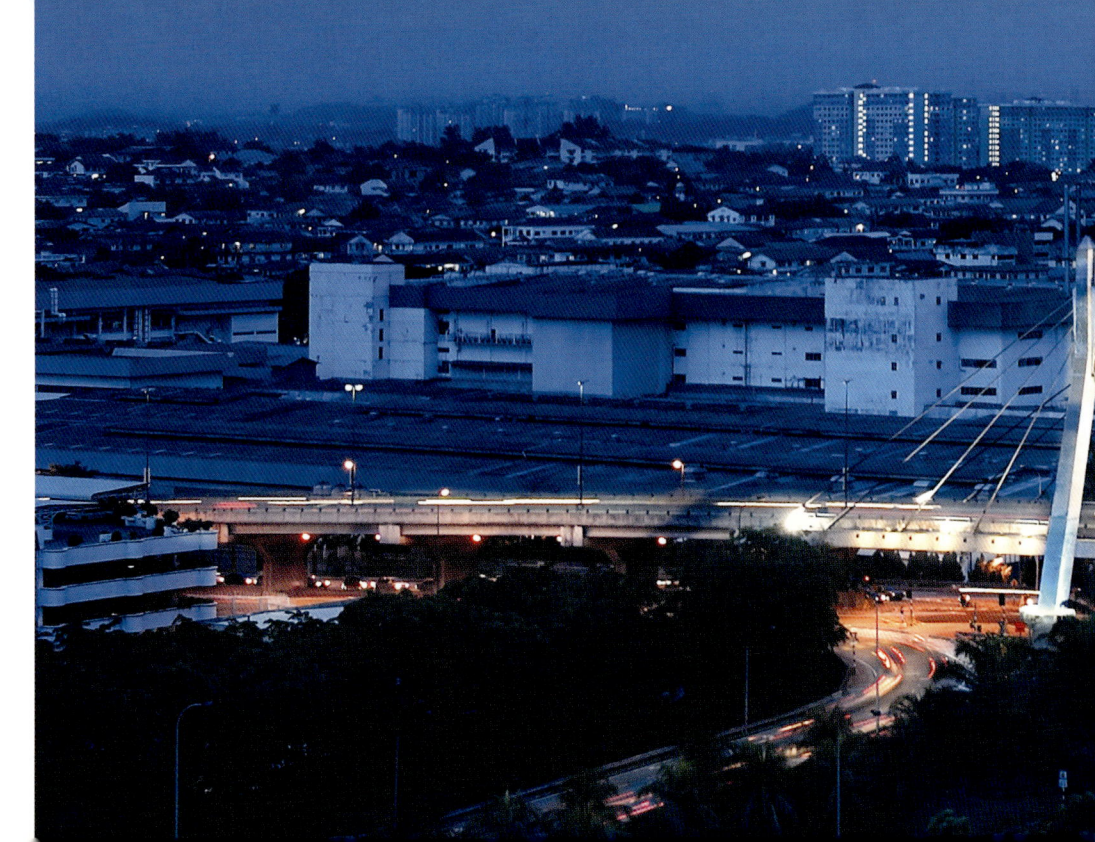

THIS PAGE The Motorola bridge, which carries the Damansara–Puchong highway across the Federal Highway, was named after the nearby factory of the electronics manufacturer. The factory has since been occupied by another company.

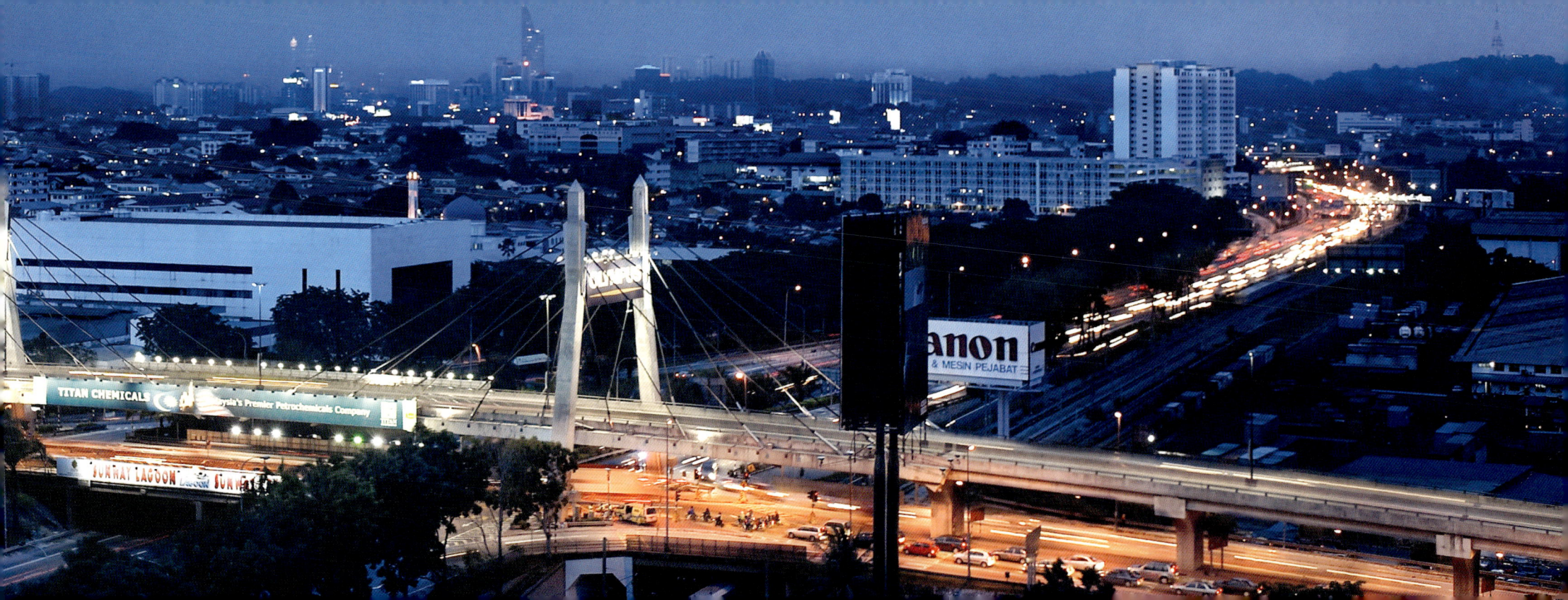

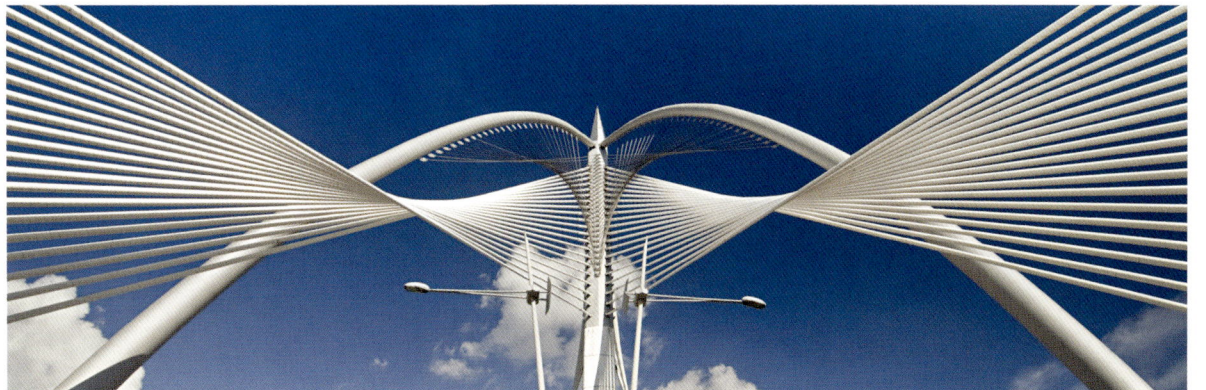
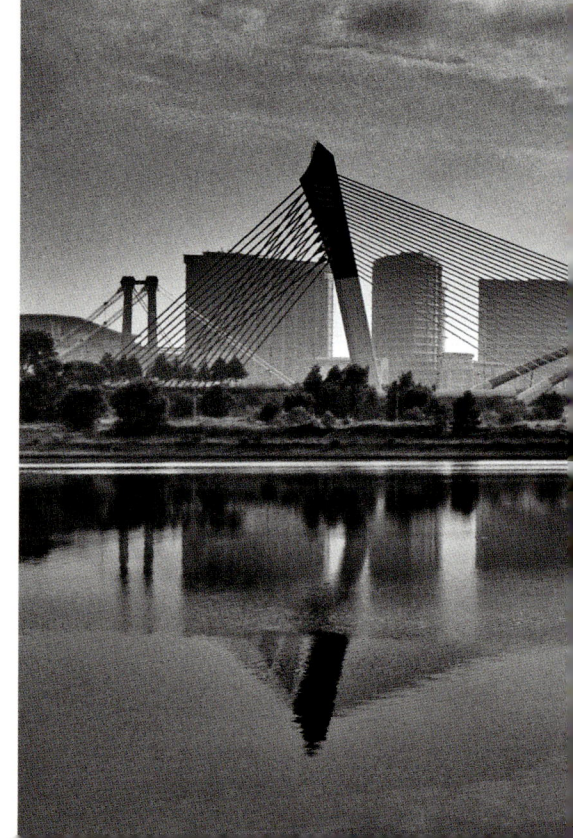

THIS PAGE AND OPPOSITE One of the newest cities in the world is Putrajaya, built from scratch entirely in the 1990s. The 435-metre Putra Bridge connects the Government Precinct and the Mixed Development Precinct. Putrajaya is also the only city in Malaysia that uses the word 'precinct'.

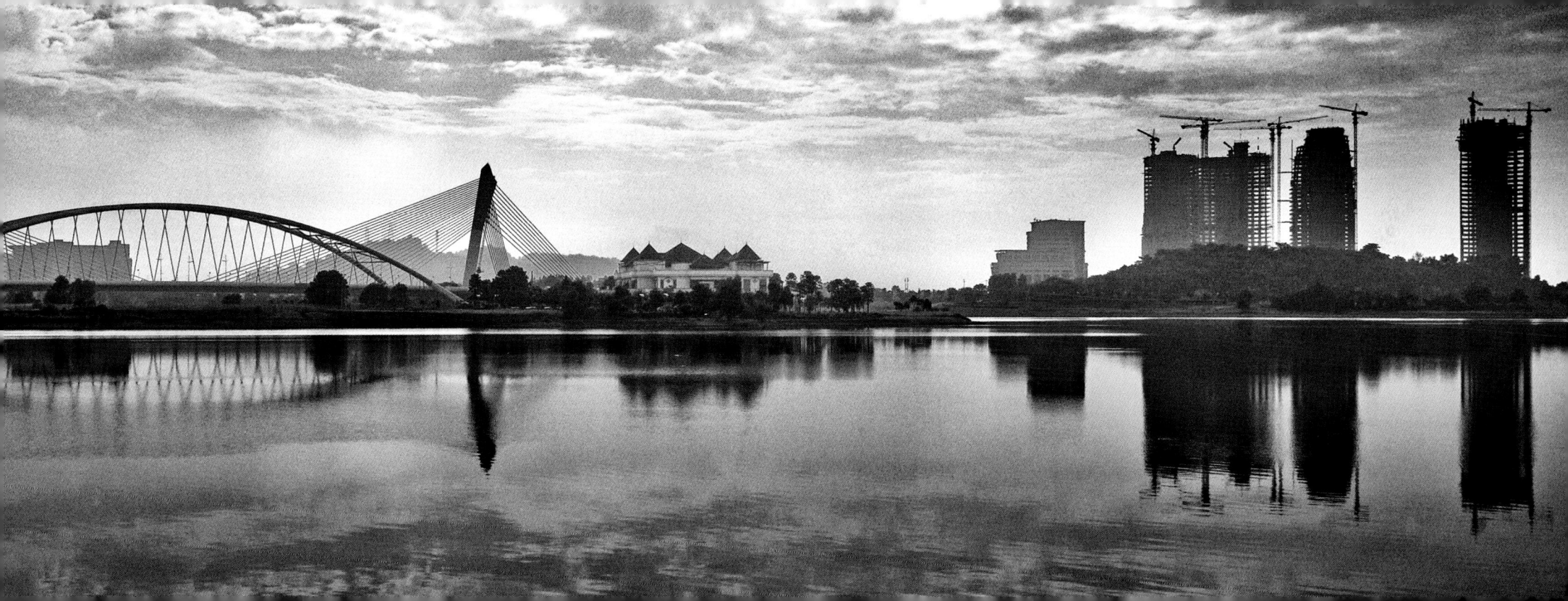

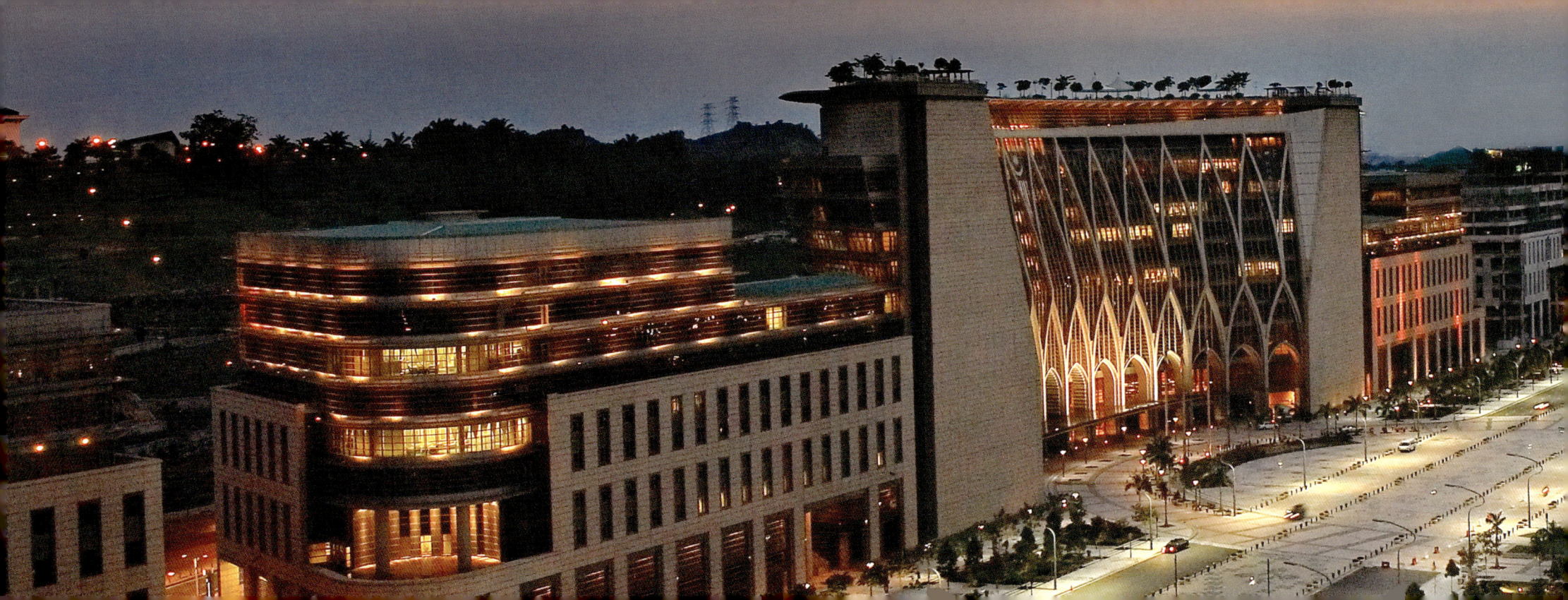

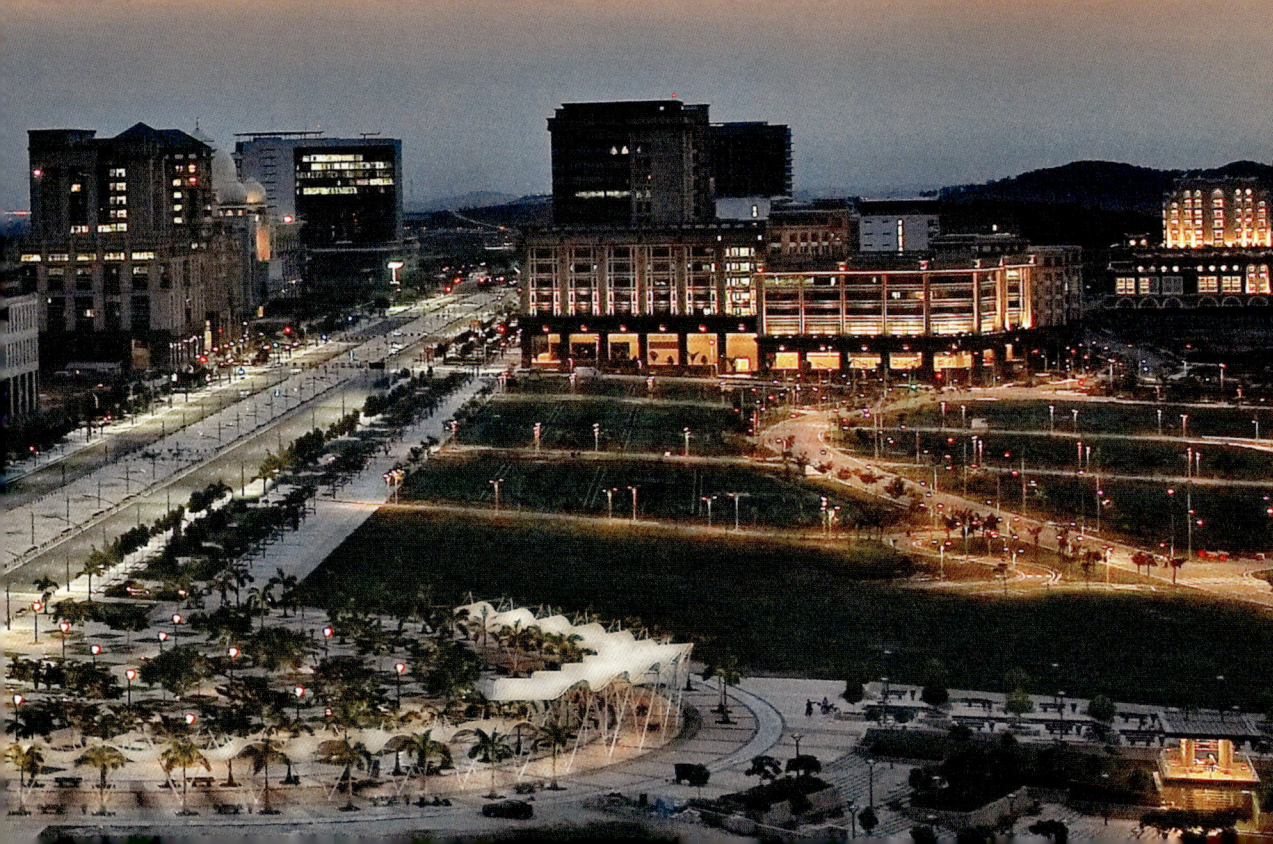

THIS PAGE Like KL, the new administrative capital of Putrajaya is a Federal Territory in its own right. Its population of 65,000 work mainly in government departments, such as the Ministry of Finance on the left. It has a much more mono-cultural (Malay) environment than KL, and is less lively at night.

THIS PAGE Close to Putrajaya is Cyberjaya (completed in 1997), a planned town carved out of an area that used to be a palm-oil plantation. It forms the heart of the MSC Malaysia, the national ICT hub. This is the view from the Multimedia Development Corporation (MDeC) building near the centre of Cyberjaya. PAGES 105–106 The TM Cyberjaya earth station. PAGE 108 Treetops of the mini-jungle at the centre of the Satellite Building at KLIA, the Kuala Lumpur International Airport.

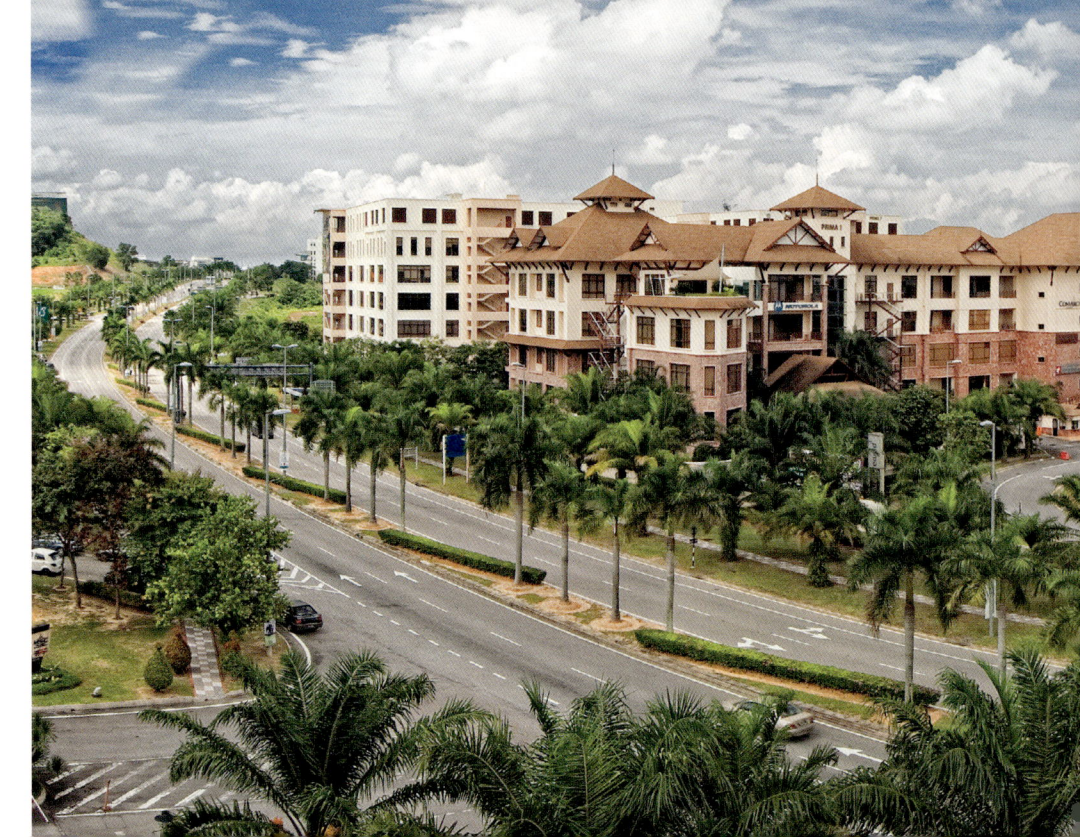

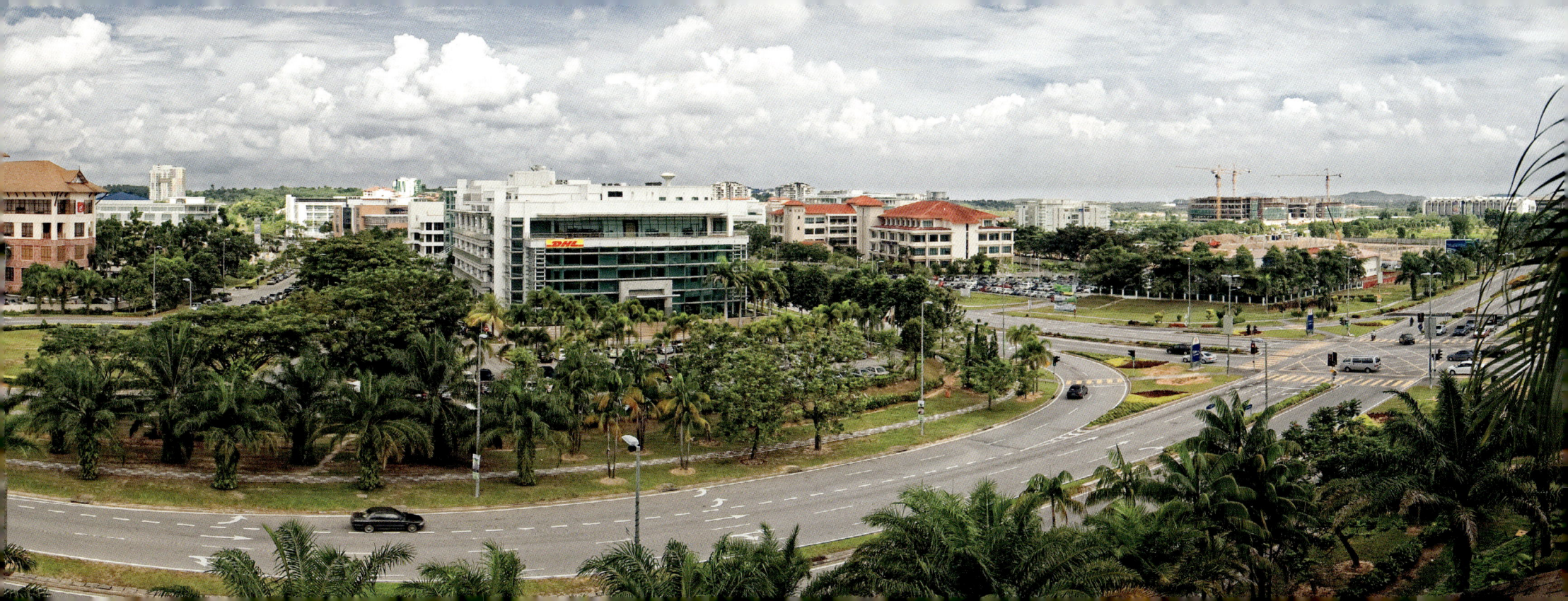

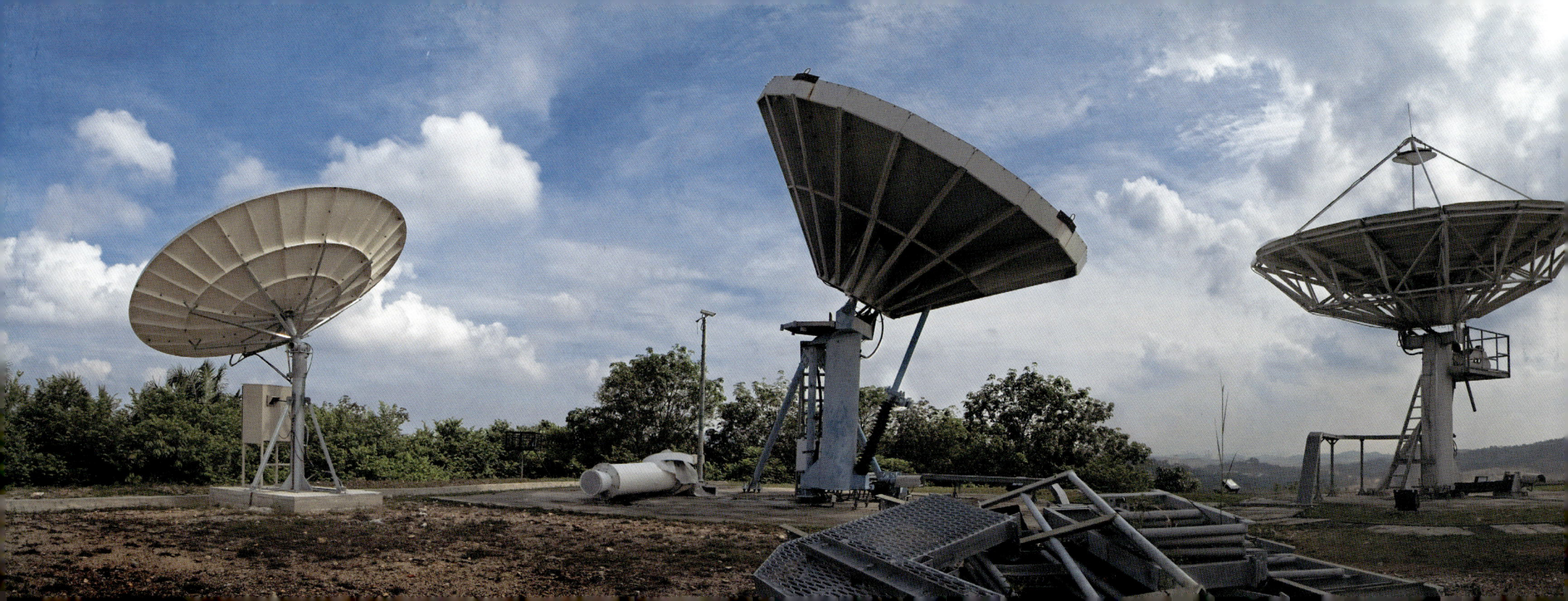

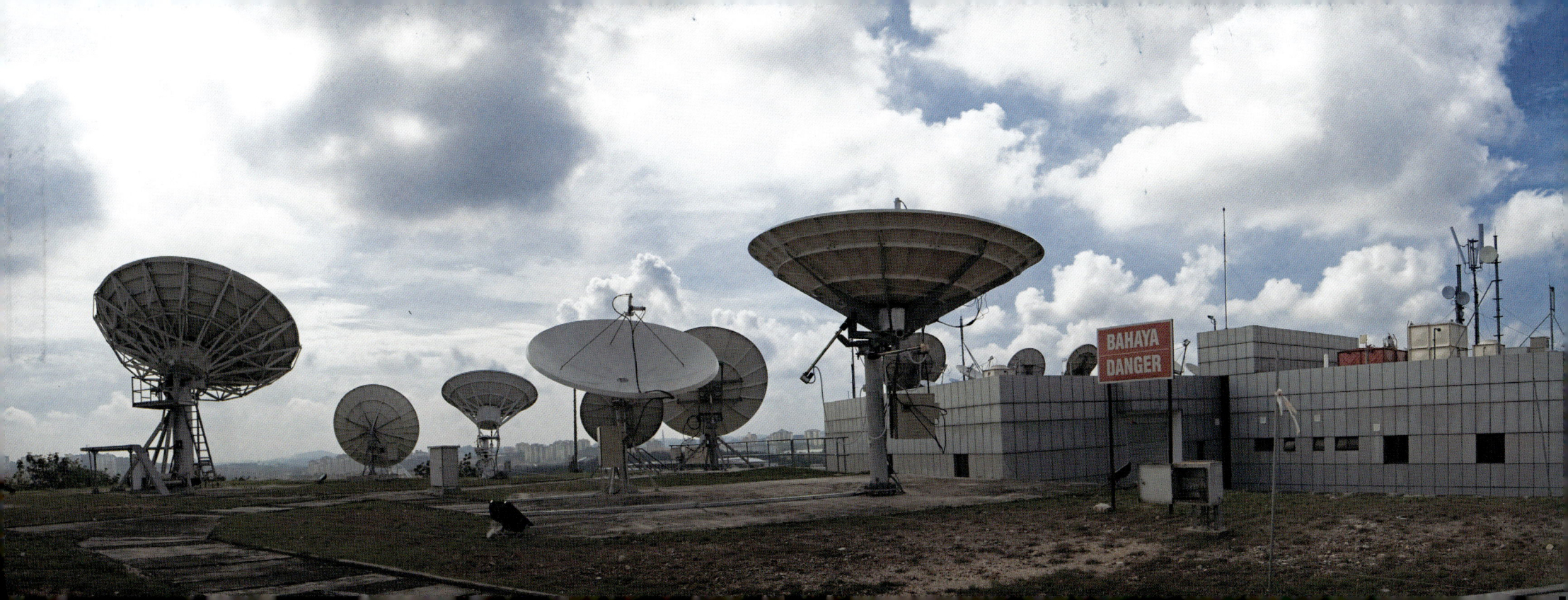

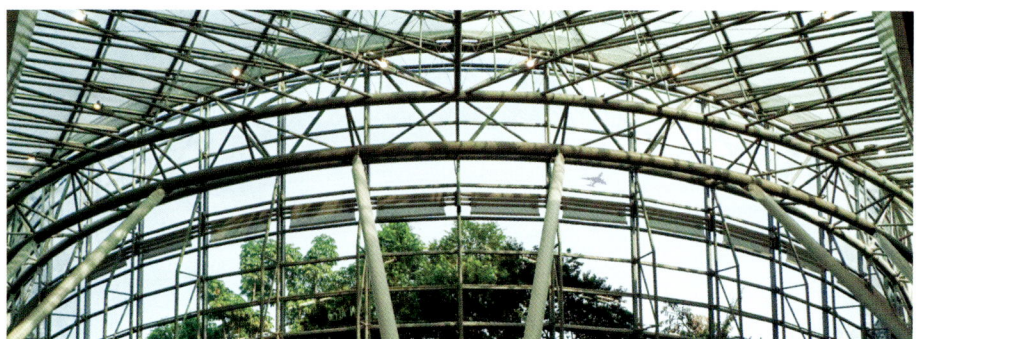

Picture Credits
All photographs by S.C. Shekar, except pp. 7, 18, 24, 31, 32, 38, 48, 52–53, 57, 60–61, 63, 68–69, 70–71, 72–73, 74–75, 76–77, 78, 88, 90–91, 93, 94–5, 96, 104–5 and 106–107 by Yee Fan and pp. 4–5 by G.R. Lambert & Co. (John Falconer).